P9-BYO-819

Curanderismo

Ari Kiev, M.D.

CURANDERISMO

Mexican-American Folk Psychiatry

THE FREE PRESS, *New York*
COLLIER–MACMILLAN LIMITED, *London*

Copyright © 1968 by The Free Press

A DIVISION OF THE MACMILLAN COMPANY

Printed in the United States of America

All rights reserved. No part of this book may be reproduced or transmitted in any form or by any means, electronic or mechanical, including photocopying, recording, or by any information storage and retrieval system, without permission in writing from the Publisher.

THE FREE PRESS
A DIVISION OF THE MACMILLAN COMPANY
866 Third Avenue, New York, New York 10022

Collier-Macmillan Canada Ltd., Toronto, Ontario

First Free Press Paperback Edition 1972

Library of Congress Catalog Card Number: 67-25331

printing number
1   2   3   4   5   6   7   8   9   10

The passage on page 15 is from an article by Professor Ozzie G. Simmons, "The Mutual Images and Expectations of Anglo-Americans and Mexican-Americans," which appeared in the Spring 1961 issue of *Daedalus* and is quoted by permission of *Daedalus* and the American Academy of Arts and Sciences.

To Phyllis

Contents

Introduction

SEVERAL YEARS AGO, I prepared an anthology of original papers dealing with the prescientific psychiatric theories and practices of some sixteen cultures throughout the world (Kiev 1964). A number of universal therapeutic techniques were delineated and found to be crucial for the success of these therapies. These findings stirred much interest, but nevertheless left unanswered the question of the therapeutic value of the specific and unique features of the particular theories and practices. The present study of Mexican-American folk psychiatry in San Antonio, Texas, was thus conceived to examine in detail the specific aspects of one system of prescientific psychiatry for the purpose of clarifying the therapeutic significance of its culture-bound elements. This study sought to determine the nature of a folk healer's sensitivity to the nuances and subtleties of psychopathology among the members of his group, and in what ways the care he offered was suitable for the specific psychopathological conflicts created in his own culture.

This investigation began with the assumption that culture creates characteristic types of conflicts that are handled in both healthy and unhealthy ways, depending on the individual, his personal history, his constitution or inherited equipment, and his life experience. We did not assume that typical cultural conflicts produce typical culture-bound illnesses or that specific culture-bound experiences cause such severe disorders as schizophrenia. Neither hypothesis could be adequately examined with the data available. We did assume, however, that the kinds of conflicts people have relate to their culture.

Culture determines what children are taught, what values are considered important, and how· major universal experiences, such as birth, life, and death are viewed. Culture also determines who will be the significant parent, methods of punishment, trends in training, emphasis in training, and so on. While biological factors no doubt set limits on the range and flexibility of human behavior in general and on specific individuals in particular, the patterns that are introduced and the directions behavioral patterns take are determined by the culture. And, as the present study demonstrates, so are the patterns of disturbance and the institutions devised to deal with them.

In this study it was possible to relate certain dominant themes and stress points in the culture to the psychopathological theory devised by the culture and employed by the *curanderos* or folk practitioners. Knowledge of these themes and stress points was obtained through conventional anthropological techniques, relying on a number of informants rather than on a large-scale survey. To understand Mexican-American culture in its most subtly complex form would have required broad-scale sampling of Mexican-American personalities; consideration of statistical distribution of certain kinds of traits; inquiry into regional differences, social class differences, and the effects of social change; and a review of the long history of the Mexican-American people. Because of obvious methodological limitations, we have tried to examine only those ethnographic facts that were significant for understanding folk beliefs and attitudes relating to psychiatric illness. Since all Mexican-Americans do not subscribe to these beliefs, we concentrated on those living in an impoverished urban area who had most apparent reason to cling to their traditional past and least contact with modern American culture. There was, to be sure, a variety of attitudes, personality traits, and beliefs even among these people, but there was enough uniformity, relative to other groups, to justify the assertion that there were certain patterns common to their way of life and way of looking at the world, as well as to their problems and methods for resolving them.

While much of our material fits into the broad category of culture-personality studies, we have not accepted the assumption that specific socialization experiences—such as the time and method of weaning and toilet training—are the fundamental experiences that shape the basic structure of the Mexican-American personality or the belief system. Rather, we have assumed that the accompanying parental attitudes toward their children are most important. A calm, loving parent is more likely to be calm and loving through all the vicissitudes of childhood training, while an anxious parent will probably communicate anxiety to the child, irrespective of the stage of development and the particular patterns of the culture. It is our view that children are tougher and more resilient than they are usually considered, and can survive various "psychological trauma" with few fixations, save where these trauma are reinforced by later experiences in the culture.

In the absence of sufficient experimental evidence and in view of the evidence regarding diverse outcomes of similar childhood experiences throughout the world, it seemed to us unwarranted to make any dogmatic assertions about childhood experiences. Without adequate sampling and observation and without considering the range of patterns of even a single parent and changes in patterns of child rearing introduced by change in family size and reduction in the assistance available from grandparents and parent surrogates, it was even more difficult to generalize. Commonly held attitudes, which are more readily obtained from field study, appear to be more critical in determining the child's attitudes toward the subsequent expression of instincts. Attitudes toward one problem in training are often more consistent with other attitudes than they are different, the constant factor in all of this being the parent. An indulgent parent may be indulgent at all stages of development and this indulgence may be more critical to the child's learning than specific techniques used. This attitude may also be conditioned by the temperament of the mother at a particular period of her life, and may at times have little to do with the cultural prescriptions regarding certain behaviors. Contributing to the mother's attitudes may be unconscious feelings of competition with the child (accentuated when grandparents ignore the mother's capabilities), problems of the father's identification with the child, and parental rejection, which may lead to maternal overprotectiveness. This, again irrespective of specific techniques, may be critical for the child's growth and development. Later experiences are also important for conditioning the individual's view of the world. Adolescence is especially important from a biological as well as a sociological viewpoint because important social experiences and the development of greater consciousness occur during this phase.

A number of different methods were employed to carry out this study. Most important was the traditional anthropological approach of participant observation. Contacts with four native healers, or *curanderos,* were made after much effort with the help of several interested Mexican-Americans. The purposes of the investigation were explained to these healers and over the ensuing months they were extensively interviewed in their homes or offices. For the most part, the data obtained are based on these interviews. Because *curanderismo* is illegal in Texas, the healers were, in almost every instance, reluctant to have actual treatments observed. Observation was possible in a few cases, however, when interviews coincided with the arrival of a patient; these observations then lent some validation to the large body of theoretical material obtained in interviews. Further validation of treatment maneuvers was also obtained by reference to several written accounts of *curanderismo* which, although focusing almost solely on physical illnesses and several magical illnesses, nevertheless described in detail the general approach to treatment used by the *curanderos.*

To supplement the anthropological data obtained from interviews, a number of patients suffering from various degrees of psychiatric illness were studied. Special effort was made to determine how these patients viewed their illnesses in relationship to the concepts of folk medicine presented by the *curanderos.* Thus, special attention was paid to whether patients considered their illnesses to be the result of witchcraft, punishment from God, or other culturally significant agents; whether they considered themselves to be suffering from a folk illness; whether they had sought the help of a *curandero;* and lastly, whether the history of their illnesses pointed to any special sources of conflict in their family and social background.

In addition, I treated several Mexican-American patients with conventional psychotherapeutic techniques during my two years in San Antonio.

To obtain additional understanding of the folk concepts of psychiatry, a series of representative case histories obtained from ward interviews, and hospital records of the State Hospital in San Antonio, and the outpatient records of the Mental Hygiene Clinic in San Antonio, were presented to the several *curanderos.* This approach provided further opportunity to discuss folk theories in a focused way and to examine more closely the approach to diagnosis utilized in this culture.

In addition to the numerous *curanderos,* patients, and informants who made this study possible, I am indebted to my friends in Texas, Henry Garcia, Doctor Daniel Saenz, Mary Esparza McGarrity, Bill Hale, and Buford Farris who helped me with the necessary contacts.

I am grateful to Lyle Saunders and Estelle Whelan who read

the manuscript in its early stages and made many helpful suggestions. I am especially grateful to Margaret Roth for her sound editorial help in the preparation of this book.

Most of all I am indebted to my wife, Phyllis Eve Kiev, whose advice and encouragement were crucial throughout all stages of this study and the preparation of this book.

ARI KIEV, M.D.

Curanderismo

1

Prescientific Psychiatry

MENTAL ILLNESS includes a large number of abnormal states of mood, thought, and behavior, ranging from mild anxiety and tension to severe, disorganizing psychosis; these states arouse a multitude of emotions in onlookers and pose threats to the harmony of all social groups. Attempts to cope with the problems of the mentally ill have been made since ancient times, but only in the last two centuries have systematic and rational psychological treatments been employed. Only in recent years has psychiatry developed into a recognized and scientific discipline.

This book is concerned with the psychological theories and treatment methods employed in the Mexican-American subculture in the American Southwest. Its purpose is to add a further dimension to our knowledge of the cultural aspects of psychiatric theory and treatment. This book focuses on the impact of cultural factors

3

on the form and content of Mexican-American folk theories and treatment, and the contribution of culture (or a group's shared system of beliefs, practices, and behavioral patterns) not only to personality formation and psychic conflict, but also to the development, patterning, perpetuation, and management of psychiatric illness.

These issues were first examined in *Magic, Faith, and Healing,* (ed. Ari Kiev, New York: The Free Press, 1964) an anthology of primitive folk psychiatries which focused on certain common elements in diverse psychological treatment approaches and on the relevance of specific cultural factors to both the content and technique of psychotherapy. One of its major inferences was that many primitive psychiatries are substantively psychological, even though they are methodologically unscientific and supernaturalistic. However, irrespective of the supernaturalist or magical methodology of primitive psychiatry, certain therapeutic factors were found to be operating in these primitive psychiatries which, on closer examination, were found also to operate in contemporary scientific psychiatries. These considerations suggested that the substantive psychology and the faith of the native healer in his system might be as important for successful treatment as the scientific accuracy of his methods. In particular, these studies underlined the emotional aspects of the therapeutic process, the nonspecific effects of therapy, the role of group forces, the powerful influence of the therapist, and the effects of cultural factors in a great range of primitive psychiatric treatments found throughout the world.

As in Western psychotherapy, it was found that in most instances the patient's favorable expectations were reinforced by the treatment setting and techniques and by the healer's faith in the patient's capacity to respond to treatment. At times, the healer's initial pessimism introduced ambiguity into the situation and increased the suggestibility and anxiety of the patient, promoting his desire to please the healer.

The connection of treatment with dominant values, by enlisting the valuable support of the community, further reinforced the

4

patient's faith in the healer or healing society and his expectation of relief.

Suggestibility was often increased by participation in emotion-arousing group dances and songs which further inclined patients to expect help. Community support, participation in healing cults, direct commands, reassurance, and environmental manipulation all were seen as realistic supportive elements which in themselves were anxiety reducing.

Possession experiences, which were encouraged in certain healing cults, and group participation provided a number of additional therapeutic benefits such as the attainment of high status through cult roles, the opportunity for acting out aggressive and sexual behaviors, the opportunity for the reversal of sexual roles, and a temporary freedom of responsibility for actions.

Psychological defenses were also strengthened by readily available belief systems by which personal idiosyncratic difficulties could be explained in terms meaningful to the group and by opportunities provided for the active expression of aggression and other pent-up feelings. Thus, analysis of institutionalized witchcraft practices which also channel aggressive drives revealed that such benefits as psychological catharsis and social control could arise from what might even be illegal and antisocial practices.

In most of the societies examined in *Magic, Faith, and Healing,* the healer utilized popular notions of his own prestige and influence. These beliefs, coupled with his special techniques, were seen as permitting him to avoid intense emotional involvements with his patients. He received institutional support for this "objective" and neutral behavior, which not only reinforced the patient's trust in the treatment, but also minimized fears of his motives. By adhering to a standardized social role, the healer gained the power of the role regardless of his personal qualities or abilities.

These studies of primitive psychiatries reveal the presence of certain factors not ordinarily emphasized in examinations of the therapeutic elements of psychological treatments. In all the societies studied, treatment procedures were governed by particular rules, and the relationships among the healer, the patient, and the group followed prescribed patterns.

One of the principal conclusions suggested by these studies was that these basic features of psychological treatment were as important as the features that differentiated them. The healer in all instances could bring a tremendous amount of personal influence to, and arouse a multitude of emotions in the patient, as well as in the group, during a healing situation. This use of influence to arouse emotion was seen to have therapeutic value. In addition, the healer's ability in most instances to use the beliefs and ideas of the group as a fulcrum for influencing successful treatment led to the reintegration of the patient into the community.

These studies were thus of special value in highlighting certain nonspecific and univeral therapeutic elements in a wide range of psychiatric systems At the same time they left unanswered questions about the specific value of culture-bound factors over and above their symbolic meaning to patients in a particular culture. Thus, while we may recognize that possession experiences, cult participation, and confession may all have a similar therapeutic value for anxious patients in different cultures, we must nevertheless determine whether they are interchangeable techniques or whether they have specific therapeutic significance only for individuals in the cultures in which they are found.

The present study was undertaken to examine these issues. In order to clarify the subtle interplay of values and customs with psychotherapeutic theory and practice, it was decided to examine the psychiatry practiced by the Mexican-American folk healers. Over the years these healers have developed an amazingly complex system of beliefs and treatments, which is subscribed to by a large portion of the Mexican-American population in the southwestern United States.* The part played by sociocultural values and forces

* Modern medical services are available and are used by Mexican-Americans. However for so-called folk illnesses as well as the vast majority of psychological and emotional difficulties, the people turn to the curandero. Thus it is not an alternative to modern medicine as much as an alternative to modern psychiatry.

in the development of Mexican-American folk theory and practice was carefully examined. Attention was paid to the role of both the patient's and the therapist's values in the receptivity or resistance to psychological inquiry. Attention was also focused on the contribution of sociocultural factors to the genesis and development of psychiatric conflict in this culture and to the perpetuation of the same, as well as to characteristic conflicts developed in this culture and the characteristic explanations and solutions provided for them.

At the outset, it should be emphasized that this is a study in ethnopsychiatry and is concerned primarily with a particular form of folk psychiatry as it has developed in connection with a specific ethnic group and with its validity for the problems and conflicts of this group. While the nonspecific aspects of the treatment are of great importance insofar as unacceptable drives and emotions are discharged here in culturally acceptable ways, they are not the major focus of this study. Rather this study focuses on the specific system of beliefs, expectancies, and practices that enable the curandero to understand and treat the problems of his patients and enable the patients to respond to the curandero. That is to say, this study is primarily concerned with the specific features of this theory and system of psychiatry that has evolved in this group and with its connections with the basic values, ideas, and conflicts that also characterize this group.

II

Mexican-Americans:
An Overview

THERE ARE TODAY some 3.5 million Spanish-speaking people concentrated in the five southwestern states. Some 400,000 are Spanish-Americans who live primarily in New Mexico and Colorado. Two million are Mexican-Americans. The remainder are Mexicans, half of whom live in Texas, where they constitute one-eighth of the state's population. These three groups, in addition to descendants of Indians from Mexico *mestizos*, and their descendants all consider themselves *La gente de la Raza*, or part of an ethnic, cultural heritage distinguished by certain shared values and attitudes and the use of a common language. This study deals exclusively with Mexicans or Mexican-Americans.

San Antonio, Texas, has long been associated with Mexican-American culture. It was named San Antonio in 1691 by Franciscan priests in honor of St. Anthony and was settled in 1718, with the establishment of missions. This settlement, named the Presidio of San Antonio de Bejar, contained some 200 settlers by 1726. In 1731, fifteen families from the Canary Islands established an adjacent colony called the Villa de San Fernando. At the time of the Louisiana purchase, San Antonio was a large settlement with a population of up to 3,000 inhabitants. It became a stop-off point for immigrants and for many who ventured further West. In 1820, it was selected as the Western outpost for Stephen Austin's community of 200 families. When Mexico gained independence in 1821, many old Mexican families returned to this city. San Antonio also was a site of numerous actions during the birth of the Texas republic in 1836 and was subject to raids from time to time even after Texas was annexed to the United States in 1846. At the time of the annexation, some 800 people lived in San Antonio. By 1850 their number had increased to 3,488 and by 1860, to 8,235 people. During these years an estimated 300 Mexicans settled in the border towns of the new state.

After the Treaty of Guadelupe-Hidalgo, ending the Mexican war in the late 1840s, some 100,000 had become United States citizens, giving the state a sizeable Mexican population. From 1861 to 1900 some 334 Mexicans annually entered the United States. This number reached a peak of 600 in 1875 and subsequently declined to less than 100 per annum by the turn of the century. This trend was altered in the first years of the century when the numbers began to increase as a result of the slow economic development and industrialization in Mexico.

During the first years of the twentieth century, it was estimated that the Mexican population of Texas increased 76 per cent. From 1910 to 1920 the increase was eight times the average increase for the six preceding decades and from 1920 to 1930 approximately five times that increase. While the earlier groups had been primarily rural in origin, laborers and industrial workers predominated in the second and third decades. (There was also a group of 25,000 political refugees who entered San Antonio following the revolution.) Immigrants were attracted by higher wages, more employment opportunities, and a better standard of living, although in some instances they were encouraged to leave Mexico for political reasons. Many who came with families were actively recruited as cheap labor for railroad repair, mining, construction, and crop harvesting. Twenty thousand came in 1910 and 100,000 in 1924. By 1930, up to a million had legally entered the United States. In 1913 large groups of Mexicans, up to 2,000 at a time, were transported by truck to the Imperial Valley. By 1920 half the migratory laborers in the Valley were Mexican, and during 1924-30 almost 60,000 a year were brought in. This increase in Mexican immigrants was facilitated by the curtailment of oriental cheap labor in 1924. By 1920, 252,000 Mexicans had entered Texas; 89,000 California; 62,000, Arizona; and 20,000 New Mexico. During the depression some 300,000 returned to Mexico, while many who remained moved to the cities to work in factories. The majority concentrated in El Paso, San Antonio, Denver, Tucson, Phoenix, Los Angeles. (Burma, 1954)

During the Second World War, immigration increased again. In 1942 an agreement with Mexico assured seasonal workers of free transportation, subsistence, and decent living quarters. In the next five years, 220,000 Mexicans entered the United States. In 1950 an additional 76,000 entered under this law, while in 1953 over 215,000 entered and in 1961 another 300,000. This *bracero* movement not only relieved some of the population pressure on the land in Mexico, but also brought an estimated 30 million dollars a year into Mexico.

In addition to those who entered legally there were an estimated one million wetbacks who entered illegally, during these same years, although nobody knows how many stayed here. In 1946 120,000 Mexicans were illegally in the border areas of the Southwest. From 1955 to 1958 an additional 400,000 were estimated to have crossed the Rio Grande into the United States, making a total between 1942 and 1955 of some million and a half *braceros*. Many who entered illegally were ignorant of immigration laws but many merely were unable to meet legal requirements or to meet the $18 immigration fee. The willingness to hire wetbacks and the expansion of the job market in the Southwest were critical elements in encouraging this illegal migration. In 1948, 90 per cent of the cotton in the Rio Grande Valley was picked by wetbacks. (Burma, 1954.)

Today 50 per cent of legal and illegal immigrants come from the states of Nuevo Leon, Guanajuato, and San Luis Potosi; the remainder, from Jalisco and Michoacan. (Saunders, 1954, Loomis, 1941.) Most are agricultural workers without their families who expect to return to Mexico after two or three months of work. Because many who leave or are deported settle in border areas, these areas become pockets of low wage-earners which provide a continuous source of new wetbacks for the United States. In addition, because established workers cannot compete with the low wages acceptable to wetbacks, many move north. Thus, many border areas have become impoverished slums containing many unassimilated people and a high potential for discrimination and ethnic conflict.

Since the 1950s the numbers coming to San Antonio have continued to increase each year, reflecting the same patterns of migration that have been noted above. Today, 60 per cent of the 500,000 people living in San Antonio and its environs belong to the Mexican-American group.

A consideration of the Mexican Revolution, changes in Mexican society, and patterns of migration to and from the United States is of importance not only in pointing to the immigrant origins of many Mexican-Americans but also in emphasizing their rural, agrarian, village background. This is particularly important because in such a background the significant values, customs, and patterns of life are considerably different from those found in an advanced, technological, urban-oriented society such as America.

The majority of Mexican-Americans derive from a background where cooperation and the subordination of the individual to the community are stressed and where such values as aggression, competition, individual responsibility, and initiative, so highly emphasized in the United States, are de-emphasized. Most come from villages that are isolated, unchanging, self-subsisting cultures, with

11

oral and sacred rather than written traditions and with little emphasis on a division of labor or the development of technology.

Helping to perpetuate the Mexican-American culture are the large numbers of immigrants from Mexico who have entered the United States in recent years. Their adherence to traditional ways have reinforced traditional attitudes among the settled population. These immigrants have little familiarity with American ways and the English language, and tend to move rapidly into the urban *barrios,* where their social contacts are limited to other Spanish-speaking people. Since education is not as valued as manual and agricultural skills, the opportunities and incentives for acquiring American values are minimized. Frequent moves, especially among migrant farm workers, further contribute to the reduced involvement in American culture, as do the deprivations associated with the relatively low social, economic, and health standards. The proximity of Mexico to the Southwest, by facilitating contact with Mexican news media and contacts with family, further perpetuates Mexican culture. Fifty thousand people cross over from Mexico to the United States each year. These people emphasize the immediate present rather than the tolerance of frustration for future benefits. Because of this cultural background and because the opportunities and channels for assimilation have never fully opened, most carry on the traditions passed down by their parents.

The handicaps of the Mexican-American group are reflected in their substandard, crowded housing, high unemployment rates, and minimal education. Four fifths of the Spanish-speaking people in the Southwest live in urban areas. In San Antonio, Mexican-Americans live in inferior, overcrowded housing with inadequate toilet facilities, pay proportionately more rent than Anglo-Americans for accomodations of comparable value, and have a high incidence of fertility, morbidity, mortality, and broken families.

While Mexican-Americans have been engaged primarily in agricultural work or in unskilled jobs, their rate of unemployment compared to the Anglo-American population has been considerable. In the number of unemployed, type of occupation, and annual income, the Mexican-Americans show all the indices of a lower socioeconomic status than the whites.

Because of a combination of language barriers, discrimination, poverty, child labor, migration patterns, and a present rather than future orientation, the Spanish-speaking people have had much difficulty in obtaining education. The primacy of cultural factors and attitudes toward education, rather than inadequate facilities, is suggested by a much higher enrollment rate in elementary schools than in high schools, where, also, there is a very high drop-out rate. This suggests that something happens in school which alters the motivation for education.

Life in these slums or shanty towns is not easy, a fact reflected not only in higher rates of family disruption, but also in the morbidity and mortality figures, as well. A comparison of twenty census tracts in the five southwestern states revealed that the Spanish-speaking had more children in families broken by death, divorce, or separation than did any other group. This high incidence of family breakdown becomes particularly significant when one considers the high birth rates in this group.

The high rate of morbidity and mortality among Mexican-Americans relates not only to the fact that they live in crowded, impoverished conditions but also to the fact that their neighborhoods often lack sanitary water supplies, insect and rodent control, sewage and garbage disposal, and adequate medical facilities. An analysis of the causes of death from 1955 to 1959 suggested that tuberculosis, infective and parasitic diseases, influenza and pneumonia, and gastritis-enteritis-colitis were perceptibly associated with Spanish-speaking concentration.

In many ways the slum examined in this study resembles other slum areas in San Antonio. Its most apparent feature is the jerry-built houses in which the people live. Some are ramshackle, poorly repaired, one-storey stucco cottages. Others are decaying wooden shacks without running water or toilet facilities. Like the *barrios, favelas, vecindades,* and *tegurios* found elsewhere in Latin America, the slum is overpopulated and crowded. The rate of population

13

growth continues to rise because of improving health conditions and the survival of more infants past the first year of life than was true a decade ago, despite the fact that morbidity and mortality are still considerably higher than in the Anglo-American group. In large measure, the slum is made up of the young and dependent with inadequate education and an undesirable position in the employment market. Thus, the slum has expanded because of high birth rates, lower child-mortality rates, and increased survival rates of the group as a whole brought about by improved health standards. It has also expanded and become overcrowded because of the influx of rural immigrants. Despite increased population growth, death rates, as noted above, are still higher in this group than in other American groups. Malnutrition and undernourishment also increase the likelihood of serious illnesses.

Psychological hazards are also great, particularly for children, because of the instability of the basic family unit. Most slum dwellers depend on contacts with family, neighbors, and employers to lessen their insecurity. Mutual aid outside the extended family is, however, limited. Participation in formal organizations is almost nil. There is a tremendous need for mother and child health services, sanitary education, mobile units for medical care, and immunization and communicable programs plus the introduction of cheap, high-protein foods. Programs of social welfare are also important, particularly for mothers of illegitimate children. Other problems include malnutrition, juvenile delinquency, the lack of primary education for the handicapped, the high incidence of childhood accidents, vagrant children, exploited child labor, child prostitution, and the persistence of certain infections with high mortality rates.

The over-all psychological attitude developed by the lower-class Mexican-American in the slum is thus greatly influenced by their nonparticipation in what on the surface appears to be a more meaningful, satisfying Anglo-American world. In that such an attitude may be considered to be grafted onto previously held attitudes and predispositions developed in the lower strata of Mexican-American society, it is easy to understand the persistence of many traits, attitudes, and customs among these people. In this connection it is of interest to consider the views of Simmons:

> That Anglo-Americans are dominant in the society and seem to monopolize its accomplishments and rewards leads Mexicans to draw the same conclusions that Anglo-Americans do, namely that Mexicans are inferior. This questioning of their own sense of worth exists in all classes of the Mexican-American group, and plays a substantial part in every adjustment to intergroup relations. There is a pronounced tendency to concede the superiority of Anglo-American ways and consequently to define Mexican ways as undesirable, inferior and disreputable. The tendency to believe in his own inferiority is counterbalanced, however, by the Mexican's fierce racial pride which sets the tone of Mexican demands and strivings for equal status even though these may slip into feelings of inferiority.
>
> The mutual expectations of the two groups contrast sharply with the ideal of a complimentarity of expectations in that Anglo-Americans expect Mexicans to become just like themselves if they are to be accorded equal status in the larger society, whereas Mexican-Americans want full acceptance regardless of the extent to which they give up their own ways and acquire those of the dominant group . . . if the full acceptance of Mexicans by Anglo-Americans is contingent upon the disappearance of cultural differences it will not be accorded in the foreseeable future . . . in viewing cultural differences primarily as disabilities, we neglect their positive aspects. Mexican-American culture represents the most constructive and effective means Mexican-Americans have yet been able to develop for coping with their changed natural and social environment. They will further exchange old ways for new only if these appear to be more meaningful and rewarding than the old, and then only if they are given full opportunity to acquire the new ways and to use them. (Simmons, 1961)

The complex of beliefs and customs associated with curanderismo is one of the main traditions persisting among Mexican-Americans. These customs have persisted in large part because of the difficulties encountered by these people in becoming a part of American society. As an impoverished, illiterate, immigrant, and minority group with a rural, agrarian background, they have been isolated from the mainstream of modern life and have developed their own subcultural world with many features of the culture of poverty. These beliefs and practices also persist because they "make sense" in terms of Mexican-American values, attitudes, personality, and conflicts. In the context of slum life in the American Southwest, curanderismo takes an added importance because of the incompatibility of Mexican-American values not only with each other but with American values. For adequate psychological functioning and for purposes of maintaining the integrity of a society, individuals develop certain expectations about the certainties of their world—in terms of both natural and interpersonal events. Associated with these expectations are certain sentiments and values with varying degrees of influence and emotional significance. Those expectations and values that lead to uncertainty or confusion or to unfavorable outcomes generate unpleasant emotions like anxiety, panic, and despair, while expectations and values leading to security generate feelings of hope and faith.

In a situation of social change, these values, sentiments, and accustomed ways of doing things are thrown into a state of upheaval, which produces emotional upheaval as well. As Frank has noted:

> In order to function successfully and enjoy life, a person must possess an integrated set of assumptions that correspond to conditions as they actually are. For it is only to the extent that a person can successfully predict the results of his acts that he can behave in such a way as to maximize chances for success and minimize those for failure. (Frank, 1961)

In a situation of social change, traditional customs and values often become obsolete and individuals are required to adjust to new values and folkways. For some, this change represents a challenge —for others, an overwhelming, disruptive emotional experience. When efforts to cope with new threats and challenges lead to failure, individuals naturally turn to those sources of comfort that were successful in combatting unpleasant emotional states in the prechange period. At the same time, the security of traditional forms is more desirable for some than the desirable features of the new. They reluctantly accept the challenge of the new, or actively resist and avoid it.

The cultural background of the Mexican-American group has determined to a large extent the nature of their adaptation to American life. The strength of the old culture plus the hostility of the new environment have led to a persistence of old customs. The interplay of these forces can be seen in such areas as child-rearing practices and social customs, which appear to be unsuited to preparing individuals for American society. The society, in turn, creates difficulty in acculturation. Resistance to social change among Mexican-Americans is related to the incompatibility of traditional Mexican values with such things as the American emphasis on education, industrial training, and egalitarianism. Adjustment difficulties in American urban areas are compensated for by the maintenance of the old social groupings and the persistence of traditional customs. Insofar as such groupings and customs have been modified and adapted to the new environment, they are less effective in satisfying individual psychological and social needs than they originally were and are unsuited for dealing with new needs. While they allow individuals to maintain a sense of ethnic consciousness and group identity, both of which maintain group norms to some extent and provides individual security through group membership, their persistence hinders complete acculturation.

This process of retarded acculturation is demonstrated by the changes in family life. Since children no longer marry in early adolescence, the period of puberty is more troublesome than in Mexico. It is especially difficult for girls, who can no longer rely on their mothers to set examples for them—for their mothers did not experience periods of sexual maturity before marriage and motherhood. Fathers, too, have difficulty understanding what their boys are doing and learning in high school at ages when they, themselves, had already specialized in trades and were bearing family responsibilities.

Changes brought about by migration to American urban areas

has led to a decline in the strength of the father's role in the family, for he is often the only family member not adapted to the new circumstances. Women are able to obtain unskilled jobs as easily as men, and can also be employed as cleaning women and domestics, giving them greater economic security than they had in Mexico, and relative independence from men. Children find some security at school. By contrast, men are often unable to find employment in their own trades, or find it difficult to learn new skills. Thus, in many instances, men are more dependent on their wives (as sources of income) and on their children (as contacts with the new culture) than they were in Mexico.

Increasing familiarity with the gadgets of Western civilization, improved sanitary conditions, and health has challenged the old order of life by making the Mexican-American more aware of his oppressed condition and of the possibilities of a better life. The increasing participation of Mexican-American children in American culture has influenced their attitudes toward schoolwork, dating, and sexual relationships which have challenged the old Mexican traditions. Women have demanded more freedom and men have been made increasingly aware of their inadequacies relative to the new standards. The wholesale adoption of many American values in the face of nonadoption of American citizenship (first-class) has unfortunately generated for many a certain kind of subcultural mentality marked by ambivalence toward American society.

Examining the significance of folk illnesses among acculturating Mexican-Americans, Madsen noted that one of the functions of folk illnesses was to provide a mechanism to avoid or to relieve situations involving a conflict between Mexican and American values. This function was especially marked in those individuals who were attempting cultural transfer, the *Inglesados*. As Madsen has written:

> The individual who has internalized values from both subcultures usually at some point becomes aware of painful cognitive dissonance. The individual's self-image loses its focus, and decision making becomes a matter of profound anxiety. The partly acculturated *Inglesado* finds identity with any recognized role in either

subgroup almost impossible. He is scorned by the conservative
Mexican-Americans and refused admission to Anglo society. Some
Inglesados in this situation seek closer identity to Anglo-culture
through such means as conspicuous display of Anglo mannerisms
or conversion to a Protestant church. Others seek to escape geo-
graphically and move to another state or to one of the larger
cities in Texas. Others attempt to retreat into the conservative
Mexican-American culture. Those who retreat are usually afflicted
with a series of folk diseases. As Anglos are believed to be immune
to such ailments, merely being afflicted by one is a means of cultural identification with *la raza*. To accept the diagnosis and to
cooperate in the treatment are a declaration of acceptance of the
conservative Mexican-American world view. The treatment
involves the re-establishment of traditional roles and frequently
some form of penance. Such treatments are nearly always con-
ducted by *curanderos*. (Madsen, 1964)

Thus, according to Madsen, folk disease represents a means of
retreat to the conservative roles of Latin society.

The anxieties and threats of cultural transfer combined with
the desire for relief may provide the psychosomatic genesis of
disease symptoms. Successful reinstatement in society and resulting
relief from physical complaint reinforce the cultural acceptance
of folk illnesses. Belief in the reality of these diseases frequently
results in the diagnosis of completely physical ailments as *susto,
mal ojo,* or one of the other afflictions in the folk system. (Madsen,
1964)

Thus, disease among the Mexican-Americans must be viewed
not only as a unique personal experience but also as a social
phenomenon with social explanations. All persistent, acute, severe,
and bizarre sickness is believed to be caused either by the punitive
action of God or by the malevolence of others. God punishes man
for neglecting religious obligations, for breaches of ritual prohibitions, or because he cannot live well with others. When social conflicts are not apparent, they are searched for, or supernatural forces
are invoked. Therapy is often a matter of reconciling disturbed
social relationships, thereby simultaneously ridding the patient of

his pathological symptoms. Thus, the folk medical systems in traditional or modified form provide channels for anxiety reduction and treatment for individuals in need.

The stereotyped diagnosis of a folk illness made by the curandero leads to a culturally stereotyped ritual, always following an accepted pattern with only slight individual variations. Only by following this prescribed pattern can the symptoms be relieved and the person reintegrated into society. Mexican-Americans say that if a person has been bewitched, he can be saved only by the curandero. Witchcraft functions here as a social sanction and those most likely to be victims are those who, by abnormal physical, social, or psychological behavior, deviate from accepted Mexican-American norms.

Direct treatment of physical symptoms is very difficult until the underlying feelings can be alleviated in traditional ways. The curandero usually recognizes at once the culturally determined aspects of each case and knows the treatment required to obtain catharsis. This cultural awareness enables him to detect the extent to which such social complications as bewitchment and fright are involved. When patients exhibit characteristic symptoms of extreme guilt and fear following antisocial acts that have invoked the use of witchcraft against them, the curandero defines a course of treatment to counteract the effects of these social complications.

Thus treatment is not merely the result of the doctor-patient relationship but is instead a form of social reintegration through socially recognized methods. Mexican folk medicine thus plays a dual role, for it is designed to maintain the continuity of society as a functioning whole as well as to reintegrate individuals into the community. Deviant behavior is eliminated by social sanctions, but at the same time, the act of elimination is part of the cycle that assures the reintegration of the individual into society.

Traditional social sanctions were designed to ensure that those who deviated psychologically from group norms would be redirected in paths of normal behavior. The deviant, whether his difference was physical or social, was likely to be thought of in terms of antisocial or witchcraft behavior. When social stress precipitated a group situation requiring some outlet for aggression, the individual who differed from Mexican-American norms was most likely to be accused of witchcraft. The accused individual could then be integrated into society by a process of confession and punishment.

When changes in the structure of traditional society and the social problems inherent in the urban environment lead to anxiety, families turn to social sanctions in an attempt to maintain the stability of the group. These traditional patterns maintain conformity with group behavior by the provision of physical, social, and psychological support for their members in forms adapted to the new society.

The penetration of American values into Mexican-American subculture has created new economic needs and new tensions in traditional social relationships, while new relationships based on trade and contract are undermining the old social structure.

III

The Curandero

THE MEXICAN-AMERICANS, who derive from a tradition-alist agrarian background, continue to lead a life whose basic assumptions and values are often at variance with the pragmatic, present-oriented, and materialist values of American society. The beliefs and customs of the curandero have persisted for much the same reasons as other values and customs, that is, because of their familiarity and utility. While their significance in relationship to Mexican-American culture is the focus of this study, it is important to note that much of the curandero's knowledge derives from traditional fifteenth- and sixteenth-century European medicine and that there are firm historical foundations for his beliefs and practices.

The curandero's beliefs about emotional illness derive in part from the Spanish-Catholic tradition of Mexico and in part from the Indian heritage bequeathed to Mexico by the Aztecs, Mayans, and other Indian groups, and are an amalgam of magic, folk belief, and empirical experience (Madsen, 1955, 1957; Foster, 1951; Holland, 1964; La Barre, 1947; Smithers, 1963). Medicine based on the teachings of Hippocrates, Galen, and Avicenna and on fifteenth-century Spanish folk medicine was first taught at Colegio de Santa Cruz in Tialtelolco by the Spanish friars (Foster, 1953). A number of them successfully classified the native botany and pharmacopoeia. Others taught humoral pathology, which was the basis of medical teaching up to the time of Mexican independence and was especially compatible with native beliefs.

Fifteenth-century Spanish medicine, derived largely from Greek and Arabic sources, was noted for anatomical dissection techniques and the study of botany (Castiglioni, 1958). Books on medicinal plants (herbals), which were used in the instruction of monks, were often printed for the laity. Many were brought to the new world by the conquerors. Anatomy texts based on the humoral theories of Galen, Hippocrates, Avicenna, Averroes, and Rhazes were also common. They supported the Hellenic notion that disease was due to a lack of harmony which nature should cure. Phlebotomy, cupping, leeching, and steam baths were common treatments, as were cautery and scarification. Food was used in treatment and a wide range of plants were used as digestives, laxatives, emetics, diuretics, diaphoretics, and styptics. Surgery was limited to wounds, fractures, dislocations, amputations, and the drainage of abscesses. Obstetrics was done by midwives and polypharmacy was commonplace. Special healing stones and amulets were prescribed for certain conditions and many believed in the value of astrology, magic, and the power of demons and sorcerers. Religious exorcism was the treatment for impotence and memory loss, and the touch of kings the cure for scrofula.

According to Galen's (138 A.D.-201 A.D.) system, the essence of life consisted of three kinds of pneumae: *pneuma psychicon* or animal spirit, with its seat in the brain, the center of sensation and movement; *pneuma physicon* or natural spirit, which arose in the center of metabolism and nutrition, the liver, and spread to the blood; and *pneuma zoticon* or vital spirit, which mixed with the blood in the heart, and which was the center of the circulation and heat regulation. Therapy by diets, exercises, massages, and climate was predicated on the formula of *contraria contrariis*. Drug therapy was largely empirico-rational, pepper being used for tertian and quartan fever, scammony for jaundice, and parsley and celery for kidney diseases.

Galen's theories were later integrated with Aristotelian biology and Hippocratic humoral theory by Avicenna (980 A.D.-1036 A.D.) in his book the *Canon* (*Q'anun*).

In thirteenth-century Spain, Arnaldus de Villanova (1235–1315) based his writings on Hippocrates and Galen, as well as on the work of the Arabs and the school of Salerno. He also wrote on the value of prayers to specific saints for specific diseases.

Several centuries before the Conquest in the thirteenth century, the idea that the mentally ill were suffering from supernatural illness became predominant. According to Zilboorg:

> If the shouting of a passage from the Bible into the ear of a patient with convulsions elicited a response, this response was proof that the illness was a demoniacal possession, because the holy words had frightened the demon. If the patient remained unaffected the illness was natural. More frequently people referred to devil sickness and witch sickness. Miraculous cures were also popular, particularly at the tombs of saints. It was during this period that the magician, the sorcerer, the heretic and the psychotic were often perceived as one and the same servants of the Devil. By the middle of the 15th century the spiritual and temporal powers had so consolidated their forces against these dangers to the Christian world that the problem of the mentally ill became a part of the codified demonology and the treatment of the mentally ill was primarily in the hands of the legal procedures. (Zilboorg, 1941, p. 139)*

*Reprinted by permission from *A History of Medical Psychology* by Gregory Zilboorg and George W. Henry, W. W. Norton & Co., Inc., 1941.

Toward the end of the fifteenth century, at the time of Columbus' discovery of America and Cortez' conquest of Mexico, the theories of Galen and Hippocrates were fused, according to Zilboorg.

> The physician of the time reasoned in a manner betraying deep apprehension that his preoccupation with clinical matters might be mistaken for indifference to the questions of sin and virtue. (Zilboorg, 1941, p. 144)*

The devil and ill humours were viewed as multiple agents in the etiology of melancholia. During the period 1487–1489, two German Dominicans, Sprenger and Kraemer, produced *The Witch's Hammer*, or *Malleus Malleficarum*, which argued that disbelief in the existence of witches was heretical. This book described ways of identifying witches and presented the legal forms of examining and sentencing a witch. As a result of this book, all those who were sick were considered to be witches, sorcerers, or bewitched. Since the *Malleus* was based on the religious belief in fallen angels, those who would not accept its premises were considered heretics. Thus, notions of insanity, witchcraft, and heresy were fused into one concept. According to the *Malleus*, the devil could injure mankind in six ways. He could: induce an evil love in a man for a woman or vice versa; plant jealousy in an individual; produce impotence; cause physical disease; cause death; deprive man of reason. According to the *Malleus*, witchcraft was the cause of illness if a physical cause could not be established, if the trouble or disease was incurable, or if it was acute.

Weyer, in his book *De Praestiggis Daemonum*, suggested that those who used poisons to cause evil to their enemies were criminals in need of punishment, but the majority of witches were innocent, sick, and in need of treatment. He set in motion an opposite trend by maintaining that witches were really people who had lost control of their emotions. He opposed the practice of obtaining confessions from witches and denied the beliefs that men could

* *Ibid.*

be transformed into animals and that witches could fly. Incubi and succubi, he said, were manifestations of anguish and apprehension, and philtres, magic, and witchcraft could never produce real ends, although they could lead to insanity. It should be noted, however, that these counter-ideas took time to develop, and that the last executions for witchcraft in Germany and Switzerland took place in 1775 and 1782. These changes had an impact on Europe but were not so rapidly transmitted to Mexico, which was cut off from the Renaissance. There, the old ideas, having fused with the beliefs of the indigenous Indian population, were widely accepted by nature healers or curanderos, who provided the bulk of medical care for the population.

In Spain, Paracelsus, who was the most influential physician during the Conquest period, argued for a rational etiology of mental illness. In his book *Diseases Which Lead to a Loss of Reason* he argued against spirit etiology in favor of the view that mental illnesses were natural diseases. He attributed epilepsy to a disturbance of the *spiritus vitae* precipitated by food or "vapor." He considered mania to be due to a substance whose vapors rose to the brain and were distilled either above or below the diaphragm. If this substance originated from excreta, the patient would refuse food, would talk to himself, would vomit, and would ignore his environment. If it were distilled in the limbs, he would be cheerful, wild, and excited. If the temperature were high, the *humor vitae* would burn and its finer particles would rise upward. The lunatic had a *spiritus vitae* which was under the influence of the moon and the stars. The *insani* were born mad because of diseased semen or because they were affected *in utero* by the moon, while the *vesani* were poisoned by food or drink, particularly food that had been subjected to the magic of love.

His treatment was empirical—camphor and powdered unicorn for "spiritual" epilepsy, incisions for mania, and the burning of waxen images for patients with excessive rage *(chorea lasciva)*. He wrote that a pregnant woman's imagination could influence the formation of the fetus, that those who kill themselves in despair are inspired by the devil, and that witches produced illness by shooting foreign bodies into the skin of their victims. In another volume, he wrote that madness could be avoided by confession and that the power of Christ, prayer, and fasting could cure those possessed by the devil. Despite this admixture of empiricism and mysticism, Paracelsus nevertheless advocated careful clinical observation and experiment and argued against the sterile reproduction of Hippocratic and Galenic notions.

Other naturalistic developments in psychiatry during the Renaissance included G. B. Da Monte's prescription of blood-letting and baths for melancholics and Mercuriale's recommendation of medical gymnastics for melancholia, which he attributed to unrestrained luxury. He described three kinds of mania: sanguineous to be treated by blood-letting; bilious to be treated by cholagogues; and melancholic for which he prescribed purgations and cautery. During this same period, Felix Plater distinguished four types of mental disease: states of mental weakness; states of activity suspension such as epilepsy, catalepsy, and apoplexy; mental alienation; and hyperexcitement.

In Mexico, these Spanish-European concepts were intermixed with the beliefs of the indigenous peoples. The Mayans, like the Aztecs, believed the world would come to a sudden end with an overpowering combination of evil influences, and much of their ritual activity focused on probing the past for clues to the future. All activities were ruled by one god or another. They attributed illness to such things as sorcery, "evil winds," and nonadherence to the ritual requirements of sacrifices or prayers. Treatments were combinations of herbal remedies and confession. Confession was made to priests, to parents, to children, or to a spouse.

Aztec religion, like that of the Spaniards, was a solar religion. The Aztecs concentrated all their aspirations and war aims on the sun, the god who was the source of life. They recognized a supreme creator and lord of the universe, whom they referred to as "the God by whom we live . . . omnipresent that knoweth all the truths and giveth all gifts . . . without whom man is as nothing . . . invisible incorporeal one God of perfect perfection and purity . . . under whose wings we find repose and a sure defense." (Prescott, 1936, p. 37) In addition to this omnipotent deity, the Aztecs had a number of other gods who were concerned with the elements, the changes of seasons, and the various occupations of man. Altogether there were thirteen main deities and more than 200 inferior deities. To each of these was consecrated a special festival or day of celebration. Indeed, all of life from birth to death was marked by religious ceremony.

While Aztec religion did not fuse ethics and spiritual perfection with religious life, and while it did not have the moral goals of Christianity, or the concepts of the Saviour, heaven, and hell, it did include many features now found in the beliefs of the curandero. The Aztecs put great store in fate and highly personalized gods, a personalism which the curandero still follows in his emphasis on the saints and personal saints. Like the curanderos of today, the Aztecs worshipped with presents, prayers, symbolic acts of propitiation, and magical maneuvers.

Like the curanderos, the Aztecs did not think in terms of the perfectability of man, but felt that the powers of the universe would determine everything. They conceived of three separate types of existence in the future life: The wicked would go to a place of everlasting darkness. Those who died of certain diseases were to live a life of indolent contentment and paradise was reserved for war heroes. These heroes passed into the presence of the sun and after some years their spirits went to animate the clouds and singing birds. When someone died, his body was dressed in the clothes symbolic of his particular deity. It was strewn with pieces of paper that operated as charms against the dangers of the dark road he was to travel. His body was burned and the ashes preserved in one of the apartments of his house.

Much as confession to the curandero is an important therapeutic measure, so too was confession important for the Aztecs. The secrets of confession were held inviolable and penances were imposed for sins confessed. As the repetition for an offense once atoned for was deemed inexpiable, confession was made but once in a man's life, usually late in life. The similarity to the curandero's technique and beliefs is clearly seen in the following passage written by Sahagun, describing the oral confession of a native.

> . . . the confessor speaks to the penitent saying: "Oh Brother thou hast come to a place of great danger and of much work and terror . . . thou hast come to a place where snares and nets are tangled and piled one upon another, so that none can pass without falling into them . . . these are thy sins, which are not only snares and nets and holes into which tho hast fallen but also wild beast, that kill and rend the body and the soul. . . . When thou wast created and sent here, thy father and mother Quetzalcoatl made thee like a precious stone . . . but by thine own will and choosing thou didst become soiled . . . and now thou hast confessed . . . thou hast uncovered and made manifest all thy sins to our Lord who shelters and purifies all sinners ; and take not this as mockery for in truth thou hast entered the fountain of mercy, which is like the clearest water with which our Lord God, who shelters and protects us all washes away the dirt from the soul . . . now thou art born anew, now dost thou begin to live ; and even now our Lord God gives thee light and a new Sun. . . . It is fitting that thou do penance working a year or more in the house of God, and there shalt thou draw blood and shalt pierce they body with cactus thorns ; and that thou make penance for the adulteries and other filth thou hast done, thou shalt pass osiers twice a day one through thine ears and one through thy tongue ; and not only as penance for the carnal sins already mentioned, but also for words and injuries with which thou hast affronted and hurt thy neighbors with thy evil tongue. And for the ingratitude in which thou hast held the favours our Lord hast done thee, and for thy inhumanity to thy neighbors in not making offering of the goods bestowed upon thee by God nor in giving to the poor the temporal goods our Lord bestowed upon thee." (Sahagun, 1946, p. 472–7, quoted in Sejourne, 1956, p. 9)*

As we shall see, the curandero has successfully fused concepts and practices from these diverse sources into an integrated and

---

* Reprinted by permission from *Burning Water* by Laurette Sejourne, Vanguard Press, Inc.

workable folk medicine. In keeping with the complexity of these several traditions and the manifold problems of the sick and troubled, the curandero must combine not only clinical skills and a thorough familiarity with a variety of empirical and ritualistic remedies, but also a piety and integrity that confirm the divine affirmation of his work. The individuals studied in San Antonio differed in intelligence, in "medical" sophistication, and in the ways in which they had become healers. One, the son of a physician, was in fact a relatively well-educated and literate man who had attended a spiritualist school in Mexico. One middle-aged curandera had attended a Catholic high school and had become a healer when she realized special powers in herself to predict the future and to read minds. The others claimed no special powers and were not literate. All had been born in Mexico. Most important, all were extremely religious people. Indeed, this facet of their lives was emphasized by them and by others in the community as the single most crucial test of their genuineness and success as healers. That this criterion was not solely a local custom is supported by the fact that Don Pedrito Jaramillo (the Healer of Los Olmos), the most famous curandero of recent times, relied solely on prayers and holy water in his successful treatments of the sick. (Hudson, 1951)

As individuals become curanderos through different paths, so too do their approaches differ. Despite predilections for somatic or psychiatric or situational problems, there is a general uniformity of views and techniques so that one may generalize about curanderismo without much difficulty.

In line with Loeb's differentiation between healers who are shamans and those who are seers, it is of interest to note that the curandero corresponds to the noninspirational seer who does not become possessed, does not exorcise or prophesy, and who does not communicate directly with a guardian spirit or God. (Loeb, 1929) While some curanderos do claim preternatural insight and the ability to forsee the future, these attributes are not essential aspects of the role. Furthermore, curanderos do not become possessed. It is of interest that in this culture there are no special initiations, dream experiences, or ordeals required to become a healer, as there are in so many other cultures. Most healers learn through apprenticeship to an older curandero, never through starvation, flagellation, isolation, or suffering. Because healing ability comes from God, abnormal mental states, either natural or induced, are not prerequisite experiences for the healer. Furthermore, the power to heal is not looked on with awe and few curanderos are overwhelmed by their own healing powers, as Devereux has noted among the Mohave. Abuse of the healing power only leads to its loss. Few become healers with the great reluctance seen in some cultures. There are indeed numerous incentives for becoming a healer, such as prestige, power, and economic reward. There are few disadvantages, because healing is not associated with schizoid or hysterical traits, which are often frowned upon, even when legitimized in special roles like healer. The symbolic accouterments of the healer's power, such as rattles, drums, masks, and fetishes, are negligible in Mexican-American culture. As healing derives from God, the curandero relies only on religious paraphernalia such as crosses and pictures of the saints. The curandero's home usually contains a large quantity of these objects as well as an altar. Most curanderos are reluctant to take fees for themselves, although they accept donations and offerings ostensibly for "the chapel" where their healing is done.

Since healing does not automatically confer charismatic powers on the healer, many rely on their persuasiveness and magnetism to arouse favorable emotions toward themselves and expectation of help in patients. Such personal forcefulness is made possible by the healer's close adherence to the religious beliefs and norms of the group. In a society where others are suspected, the religious healer's motives are unchallenged and trusted. His knowledge, intuition, humility, and interest in people may be important, but his religious demeanor, untrammeled by the authority of the Church, is his paramount virtue. While his reputation depends upon his successes, he is not blamed for his failures because the group accepts the role of God's will in all matters of health.

31

Curanderismo

In early stages of illness, individuals treat themselves or are treated by family members with knowledge of home remedies, If no relief is obtained, they seek someone with greater knowledge. If this, too, is unsuccessful, a paid specialist in herbs, or *herbolario*, is consulted. If he too fails to bring relief, a family counsel may be held to determine what to do next. Most Mexican-Americans in the barrio in San Antonio visit American clinics and doctors, especially for school vaccinations, job certificates, insurance examinations, and illnesses requiring immediate hospitalization. For minor illnesses, chronic untreatable conditions, functional illnesses, and other conditions which arouse considerable anxiety and which they fear may be supernatural, the majority prefer to rely upon the curandero. Curanderos may, however, be seen at all stages of all illnesses, depending upon the nature of symptoms, the availability of other sources of help, the particular beliefs of the people concerned, and the anxiety level. Even those who are skeptical of the folk beliefs are likely to think of the curandero when recovery from illness is delayed. Curanderos are sought after most often for serious, febrile illnesses of children, convulsions, apathy, and socially disruptive and disturbing symptoms, as well as chronic nonremitting illnesses or symptoms.

IV

General Views of
Illness and Health

BEFORE EXAMINING the specific syndromes treated and the methods of treatment used by curanderos in the southwestern United States, it is useful to describe some of their general views of illness and health, and thereby to establish a framework in which the more specific details can be better understood. These general themes represent a composite of the views of the four curanderos who were studied. It is important to note that they are views to which the vast majority of Mexican-Americans in the slum subscribe. (Bourke, 1894; Clark, 1959; Erasmus, 1952; Schulman, 1962)

Religion is the central focus of the curandero. He accepts life as ordained by the divine will, and believes that good health and happiness are given only to those who keep God's commandments. While this view encourages resignation and passivity and discourages efforts to change the world, it also provides a sense of security and comfort for the curandero and his patients in the face of illness. Men are believed to be born as sinners, a belief which supports the notion that suffering is a part of life. Death, too, is viewed as evidence of this sin. Even when a curandero uncovers specific causes of illness he is still likely to focus on sin and the will of God as critical factors which have affected the susceptibility of the patient and predisposed him to illness.

When illness occurs in a religious and pious person, it is rationalized by the belief that God allows men to suffer in order to learn. Even when prayers fail to restore health, illness is attributed to His purpose and plan for man and is never questioned, for to question would mean that the curandero was challenging God's plan for the universe. A patient who tolerates suffering is thus seen as helping God to achieve his purposes on earth. The suffering of the innocent is seen as part of this plan, for all men are expected to share the joys and the sorrows of their fellow men. Thus, the individual patient's plight is a family affair, and sometimes even a community concern because his suffering is not wholly personal but meaningful for other "children of God."

By recognizing that the Mexican-American believes that another's suffering is symbolically his own, one can understand his skepticism of American medicine, which emphasizes the patient, sometimes to the exclusion of family and friends.

The ability to suffer is a measure of an individual's faith in God, and the curandero sees his major task as helping his patient accept this suffering as his share of the burden of the world's sin and ignorance and as his part in God's world. Thus it is that the validity of a curandero's claims rest in large part on the extent of his basic devoutness and piety. The more religious he is and the more he can help others to accept their suffering and accept the will of God, the better healer he is thought to be. The prevention of human suffering is not an end in itself, for this would mean altering the basic pattern of Mexican culture. The individual would suffer even more, were God not causing some to suffer as he allowed Christ to suffer.

The theme of Christ permeates much of the curandero's thinking about illness. When he tells his patients about Christ on the cross, he encourages them to feel that they are doing what Christ did, dying so that others might live to enjoy grace. At times he may encourage them to see the experience of illness and suffering as worthwhile for those around him, for suffering increases their sense of sympathy, compassion, service, and love, as well as self-sacrifice, courage, and heroism.

The curandero and his patients view illness in this religious and social context, not in the medical-scientific one of Anglo society. Illness is not a chance event but is inextricably bound to the religious history of the individual and his group. This belief takes on special significance in the slum, where many have abandoned tradition. According to the curanderos, the younger generation has lost touch with the wisdom (folk) of preceding generations and with the values of the Church and family. Particularly criticized are the fact that mothers seek employment outside the home, children have little direction and supervision, illegitimate births are frequent, and crime is rife. Those who grow up in such a setting, with few traditional boundaries and values, get "an enemy in the brain" which prevents them from believing in anything or following the Church, and prevents them from developing those qualities of character which make people free of mental illness. Changes in traditional patterns of life are felt to violate God's will, and as such are a source of potential difficulty. The adoption of the materialistic values of American society is also opposed, as is the American idea of the equality of the sexes, which has challenged the traditional Mexican-American family and made women discontent with their lot. According to one curandero:

> More people leave their families now than did in the past—
> it used to be the custom that the girl would not go too far from
> her parents. Sometimes, nowadays they get married and they

just take off . . . well, some parents can't stand for this. They just sit at home and feel bad about it. The outsider came and interfered with their son or daughter. If they stay close, they just feel they have gained a son or a daughter. Children don't take care of their parents as much as they did before, they are too much interested in themselves and their good times. The only thing they use them today for is to baby-sit for them.

The roots of illness are thus attributed in part to the pattern of life and the values emphasized in Anglo society, which violate the religious values of a family-centered, static agrarian society. The economics of urban living stand out as a crucial deterrent to family stability. The curanderos are quick to point out that when women work, they cannot comfortably return in the evenings to care for their families; they are not in good humor and they are reluctant to work around the house. When families get too big, wives often desert them because their husbands, who are irregularly employed, cannot support the family. Women are further frustrated by their husband's extra-marital activities, part of the *machismo* complex, which is not as accepted here as in the agrarian communities of Mexico. As a result of the loss of significance and the isolation of the family from the community, and the lack of satisfaction in fulfilling old roles, there is adultery among women as well as men, which further adds to the disruption of the family. As one curandero said:

Mental goes by the spirit of the body. The mind is governed by the spirit of the body. If the body feels something the mind is affected. Deliria depends how you were born and the people surrounding you. People envy you and therefore you are sad. Start thinking it is true what they were thinking. You have many friends, they do everything different, live different, good friends, they do something wrong, everything, then talk about you. If you've got a sweetheart, love her too much, see the effects. Family doesn't want her because she is attractive and stupid. Start worrying if you get deliria. See a girl and like her, if she has all you want and everybody likes her, rich or poor, they want her, then you get near her, fight each other, have a different life. People bother you because they want her. If you get near the girl they kill you. You delirious because they follow you. Married woman, husband lets them loose, and has a party with men and women, she tries to make love with somebody, doesn't do anything wrong, you are jealous. You and her start fighting, husband has it in his mind, begin to think and they will harm him. Jealous husband's eye looks at man who gets sick because of fear. Woman is jealous of her husband, she gets sickness of mind too. When they are young they have lots of problems, we don't feel the problems until we get old. If you are strong and healthy, you've got good mind and spirit. Sometimes hardships of life and start thinking differently.

Mind is like a rubber, sometimes you think about big, sometimes little things, or worry too much or too little. Sometimes you get sad from broken heart, you are desperate, discontented, and you suffer inside after the death of a loved one. Sometimes you get sad if you are married and you see your brother look at your wife, you don't like this way. Not happy, always desperate, don't like nothing, keep it inside all the time. Mad, fussy, irritable.

While not all families are seen as disorganized, all save a few are believed to be exposed to the temptations and stresses of urban American life, which increases their risk of illness and suffering. Good health implies that an individual is in good balance with God and with the customs of the people, which focus around the family, the Church, and one's fellow man. When traditional patterns of behavior are disrupted, the individual is more susceptible to the development of bad habits, conflicts, and trouble, a susceptibility increased by his inclination to stop living a healthy, God-fearing life. Changes attendant upon immigration and urban living, such as the breakdown of the family, the changing role of women, and the changing standards of child socialization techniques (especially as regards discipline and respect) are seen by the curandero as major factors in increasing the susceptibility of individuals to illness.

These crudely formulated sociological hypotheses are of interest because of their close correspondence to the numerous theories of psychiatrists and social scientists about the deleterious effects of migration and acculturation. There is a difference, however, which should be emphasized. This is the belief that life in the urban slum is unhealthy not only because it disrupts the family and exposes people to new stresses, but also because it runs counter to traditional religious values and to the will of God. This is believed to be the fundamental factor producing psychological and behavioral disturbances. The curandero's role in the urban slum is critical, since he represents a link with Mexican traditions and can interpret contemporary problems and conflicts with a time-tested religious ideology, which has meaning for others of his group.

Since the curandero conceives of man as being made up of an evil as well as a divine side, he has little difficulty in relating changing customs and patterns of behavior to his traditional orientation. It is believed that most men cannot tell whether evil promptings come from their own nature or from the suggestion of an alien spirit with a perverted will. While this knowledge is important it is not necessary, since the avoidance of sin is the thing that really matters. According to most curanderos, the avoidance of sin is always within the power of men, through the grace of God and the help of the Holy Spirit. The devil can enter a man's life only when he voluntarily veers away from the moral order or displays weakness through carelessness.

The acceptance of both good and evil influences is supported by the belief that matter can pass through matter, and that mind can influence matter. It is also supported by the beliefs that words and wishes have creative power, that communication with the dead is possible, and that the dead can influence life on earth. These folk beliefs rest on the assumption of mysterious forces in the world, which can provide certain individuals with special powers to cause and cure illness and death. Working through *brujas* (witches) and sorcerers (who are sometimes called black curanderos), the devil is able to cause a variety of physical and mental illnesses. *Brujas* derive their power from pacts with the devil or from a more powerful witch, such as a bearded man-goat who leads a witches' circle. These beliefs are supported by the Bible's reference to the devil having received permission from God to use the spirits of the dead. *Brujas* are bound to the pacts they have made with the devil, and failure to adhere to such pacts may lead to a loss of spirit and possession by an even worse spirit, or to death for them. Because the *brujas* and sorcerers are bound by these pacts, many look upon them as "poor devils, who cannot control their own fate." Some have been seduced by temptation and forgotten God, and thus are not responsible for their own fates. The sorcerers are believed to have special powers and knowledge, and are objects of fear.

In general, however, they do not live long, particularly when they lose their power by excessive dancing, drinking, and womanizing. As long they live, they are protected by magical words and objects, but they can lose their power by disobeying the devil or by doing good deeds.

Brujas can cause illness by stealing the heart of their victim, or by shooting objects into the body. (Senter, 1945; Senter, 1947; Hawley, 1946; Parsons, E. C., 1927; Hurt, 1940) They gain access to the evil side of men through prayer, ritual, and symbol much as religious people gain access to God. They use magical words and gestures to call upon supernatural powers, and can also control the actions of ghosts, thereby harming others. They can use silent or spoken curses to harm individuals or bring bad luck to them. Some use image magic and obtain hair, feces, urine, sputum, or menstrual blood from the intended victim, imbue it with evil powers, and bring it in contact with the victim. Cursed herbs or a decoction of poison may also be put into the victim's food or drink. They can change a ghost into any animate or inanimate object, which, when in disguise, can contact any one to cause him harm. Illness caused by spirit possession is supported by the belief that the soul is usually not reconciled to its fate immediately upon death and may wish to enter another body or may wish for another's death so as to have a companion in the spirit world. The people especially fear the ghosts of those who died without earthly fulfillment, such as young children, brides, or women in childbirth, for they are most likely to be dissatisfied and envious of the living, and thus easily manipulated by the *brujas*.

As we shall see when we examine the data on specific psychiatric syndromes, the witch theory is more often relied upon for an explanation of etiology than is the set of religious conceptions we have described. Before discussing syndromes it is of value to consider the significance of this different usage of beliefs. Why is there a need at all for this additional witch theory, when the religious beliefs not only seem sufficient but correspond to what we have seen is a passive-dependent, fatalistic orientation of the Mexican-American. Psychodynamic formulations are particularly useful in helping us to answer this.

The evildoer's mystique and power develops from the fact that he does exactly what the culture does not condone. By acting in a way prohibited to others he can vicariously satisfy the unconscious fantasies and needs of his fellow-villagers. The ambivalence toward the sorcerer as displayed in both fear and fascination of him is due to this. Others identify with his lack of inhibitions but at the same time are afraid of coming under his control and losing control of their own repressed sexual and aggressive drives. That this is so is supported further by the fact that illness caused by witches and sorcerers is associated with loss of control. At the same time loss of control, or impulsiveness, is usually considered to be a manifestation of illness and is attributed to the witches. That the witch theory and other magical beliefs are related to problems of expression of sex and aggression has been recognized for some time. Erikson has written:

> The belief in demons permitted persistent externalization of one's own unconscious thoughts and preconscious impulses of avarice and malice as well as thoughts which one suspected one's neighbor of having . . . .
> . . . In all magic thinking, the unknown and the unconscious meet at a common frontier: murderous, adulterous, or avaricious wishes . . . are all forced upon men by evil-wishing neighbors . . . .
> In a world full of dangers they may have served as a source of

security, for they make the unfamiliar familiar, and permit the individual to say to his fears and conflicts, "I see you! I recognize you!" (Erikson, 1958, p. 60)

The attribution of active, aggressive, changeable, and seductive characteristics to witchcraft parallels the denial of comparable needs in the Mexican-American. Behavior motivated by such needs is discouraged or punished in childhood. The fear of retaliation by *brujas* for expressions of hostility, autonomy, emotion, and envy stems from the socialization stress on constraint, dependency, and the child's experience of inconsistency which leads him to a basic mistrust of others.

Many individuals are motivated early by an exaggerated fear of others and of the world, reinforced by the cultural beliefs about spirits and witches. Aggression problems are especially related to these fears. A child is indulged initially and later is partially rejected in favor of another sibling. As we know, over-indulgence provides little training in self-control. The child grows up ill-prepared to restrain his aggression, but aggression is a cardinal sin in Mexican-American eyes. Fears of losing control and expressing aggression provoked in a somewhat overbearing, partly rejecting childhood experience must thus be resolved. The projection of this aggression onto culturally acknowledged symbols and objects such as witches would appear to be one resolution, in that the witch becomes the source of aggression, an individual's fears are legitimized, and, at the same time, he is given an acceptable explanation or "out" should he actually lose control. Furthermore, by engaging in various antiwitch activities, he is given opportunity to express aggressive feelings.

Belief in witches also provides a cultural medium through which illness can be "expressed." In many cases, a pathological fear of witches can itself bring on illness. Any Mexican-American who suffers from certain illnesses will believe himself bewitched, but not all Mexican-Americans are so afraid of witches that the fear drives them to sickness. As we shall see in more markedly paranoid individuals, intense fear of others is expressed as fear of witches.

41

Paranoid traits and cultural beliefs in witches obviously reinforce each other. When a person feels ill, he suspects witchcraft, which in turn aggravates his illness.

Writing of the Cochiti, Fox has said:

> . . . Paranoia may be at the root of the witch illness complex. . . . Even if the primary cause of the illness is "physical" the fear of witches engendered by it produces secondary "mental" symptoms that serve to intensify it. An individual is either to some degree paranoid with stress inducing physical illness or he is physically ill which induces a state of acute paranoia. In either case the paranoia must be dealt with and the witch theory offers a medium for the expression of the illness and explanation of its cause and through the societies, a means for its cure. (Fox, 1964, p. 195)

These brief remarks indicate that a belief in witches is strongly related to early socialization experiences and the patterning of certain traits. In Mexican-Americans the belief is first associated with certain anxieties which serve to explain certain illnesses. Later, these ideas not only continue to function as projected sources of anxiety and aggression, but take on an anxiety-producing function as well. Thus in some situations it is difficult to know whether the witch fear is a defense against experienced anxiety or the cause of anxiety. Careful consideration of the witch complex suggests that it is indeed both. It functions very much as a psychiatric symptom which is both a defense against underlying dynamic conflicts and, particularly when it is not successfully reducing anxiety, the source of anxiety and discomfort.

In addition to the preceding religious, "sociological," and supernaturalistic views of illness, a strong naturalistic element is also to be found among the curandero's beliefs that is in line with the Hippocratic and Spanish Renaissance medical traditions from which they derive. Most important, the curandero recognizes the importance of adequate amounts of food, water, and air for good health. An excess of food, an improper mixture of food, or the ingestion of food which is too strong and indigestible are thought to cause digestive disturbances. This is because the heat of digestion is insufficient to digest all the food when excess food is eaten, and the residual food produces abdominal pain. Indigestible substances also hinder digestion by producing residuals which in turn produce gas, which rises and produces various symptoms. This last phenomenon relates to the belief that health results from the free passage of air and disease results from its obstructed passage. Obstruction leads to the accumulation of residuals that produce *aires*, which cause diseases. Changes from excessive heat or excessive cold also affect these *aires* and may activate a dormant process or may heat or chill the bile or phlegm, thereby producing illness. Furthermore, the same cause may produce a different illness in two different people depending on their particular susceptibility. The same illness may sometimes be produced by different external causes.

Health is the result of perfect equilibrium between these internal humors and *aires*, as well as between man and his family, and between man and God. Bad nutrition upsets the balance as does drainage of a humor, while humors are renewed by food and water. Fever is produced when the body has a surplus of undigested food, when new food is eaten, or when the individual is constipated. Heat is the force that generates the humors from food, keeps them in motion, and restores a disturbed balance. In the newborn, the heat of the heart is greatest because the body has to grow. Thus, fevers in old people are not as acute as in young people. In winter and spring the bellies are hotter and people sleep longer. In these seasons one has to eat more because the innate heat is more abundant and more food is needed. The notion of heat relates to the belief in the body's natural healing power, which restores lost balance.

If the liver or saliva dry up as happens with "rocks" in the gall bladder, the balance is also upset and symptoms of bad taste and tension may develop. To maintain a sound mind, an individual's kidneys and bowels must function normally. Stopped-up bowels may lead to rheumatism or to a stroke through straining. An unnatural balance of basic elements may lead to a loss of hearing, as occurs with water, air, or pus in the ears, or the entry of air into other body cavities. Too much wind, storm, flood, lightning, and sun are believed to be deleterious. Abnormal habits are also believed to be deleterious to health. Fellatio and cunnilinctus, for example, "suck out one's strength" and lead to a loss of control of body and mind and insanity; marrow is drained from the bones and tubes, leading inevitably to loss of sexual control, impotence, or premature ejaculations. From abnormal sexual practices a woman may lose her strength, develop a "cold" womb, and be unable to have children.

Frequent physical examinations of the rectum and the excessive use of enemas may accustom a child to this particular sensation and predispose him to homosexuality, while masturbation can lead to a decrease in strength and sometimes to insanity. Excess sexual activity and improper nutrition may produce a desiccation of the nerves, while inadequate sexual gratification may produce insanity. Nymphomania, mental and physical retardation, and hydrocephalus are thought to be secondary to syphilis, which in turn is thought to come merely from physical contact. These naturalistic theories are inextricably associated with the religious and supernatural explanation described above. Thus, God punishes man not only for violating the moral standards of the group, but also for excesses. Too much smoking, too much sexual activity, and other violations of the way of nature lead to punishment by God.

While some of these hygienic prescriptions appear reasonable, others are clearly superstitions, such as the belief that urinating in a fire may lead to decreased virility, the belief that washing one's hair during menstruation may lead to death, and the belief that violation of nudity taboos may lead to blindness.

Heredity, a preoccupation with sexual activity, and pica (or *comotierre*) which leads to obstruction of the gastrointestinal tract through the formation of boluses (*la moheca*) are other causes of insanity. Through these various beliefs runs the major theme that the misuse of one's body, given by God, is harmful. Over-exposure to the sun causes a fire in the head which produces insanity. Sexual relations only one half hour after a meal instead of three hours later can lead to paralysis, as can bathing immediately after eating. Excessive or dammed-up sexual energy may lead to epilepsy or insanity, as may excessive guilt, worry, or fear. Of interest in this connection is the belief that dreams offer a path of discharge for these emotions, and are necessary for good mental health. The cessation of dreaming is interpreted as a loss of intellect.

Death in the family, failure in love, old age, and a failing constitution can also contribute to an imbalance of humors through the excessive accumulation of strong feelings such as fear, sadness, shame, hostility, and jealousy. The role of the group is especially important, for it is believed that some people make others sick by reminding them of unpleasant memories, while others make them well through their supportive manner. The group is also important in maintaining morale. A hospitalized patient without visitors may get sad and become crazy. Sudden changes in an individual's habits and way of life expose him to great risk by creating many emotions which are difficult to deal with. Sudden poverty leads to great sadness while sudden wealth exposes the individual to the envy of others and may lead to *embrujada*.

The importance of these various beliefs is demonstrated by the extent to which they are considered by the curandero in preventing illness. In addition to measures required by Anglo law (e.g., compulsory vaccination), there are a number of traditional magicoreligious and hygienic practices used by the curandero, who is not inclined to accept illness as a chance event. He continually insists that his patients and their families attend Masses, learn the Catholic catechism, pray for good health, and adhere to the strictures of the faith. He also expects individuals to live in accordance with principles of good community living and good moral character and to avoid situations leading to jealousy, anger, and envy, which exert a deleterious effect on mental health and hence on physical health. This tie-in of religion and illness is reinforced by the belief that the violation of religious and social principles may lead to punishment by God in the form of illness. In that the dead may be used by the devil, funeral preparations are carefully made to insure that the dead soul will get to heaven and not linger on the earth, causing illness and death among the living. Many people wear charms, rings, or emblems to placate the dead and discourage their return.

Hippocratic notions play a large part in beliefs concerning prevention of illness. According to Hippocrates, each of the bodily humors was characterized by qualities associated with fire, earth, water, or vapor. Blood was hot and wet, phlegm cold and wet, yellow bile hot and dry, and black bile cold and dry. The balance of these humors and their qualities was the essence of good health, while illness was characterized by extremes of these properties of hot and cold, dry and wet. According to the curandero, illnesses may be considered as cold or hot illnesses, irrespective of the presence of fever. Individuals must consider the state of their being before eating or drinking, since if one is overheated he must avoid hot liquids and must take cold ones. An overheated individual, however, must avoid a draft or breathing cold air lest he catch cold. He must not eat certain hot foods with certain cold ones. People are also advised to keep their stomachs clean by using purgatives and laxatives regularly, and thus to avoid rheumatism and the development of strokes from straining. Cold air and ventilated rooms, which may produce *aire* are advised against, as are grapefruits which are believed to thin the blood.

Osha, or wild parsley, is used as a protection against rattlesnake bites. It is also a good prophylactic against *aire* and colds and wound worsening, or *encono*, (increased pain and discharge in a wound brought about unwittingly by someone with the special power to worsen wounds.) Sometimes the curandero will give an individual a little sack with *osha* in it to be worn around the neck as a charm. Occasionally he may give them a little sack containing garlic, or *ajo*, religious medals, or a red ribbon, all of which serve protective purposes. During pregnancy he prescribes special diets and exercises and advises against room light. Most curanderos also emphasize a number of other precautions. During an eclipse the pregnant woman must hang some keys around her waist lest the baby be deformed by the moon's shadow. Women must also be cautious with regard to the amount of water they drink, lest the head of the fetus becomes too large to pass through the birth canal. During pregnancy hot foods are avoided lest the child suffer from diaper rash after birth. Certain cold foods like fruit juices, tomatoes, pork, and certain vegetables are avoided after birth because they are too cold and their ingestion will lead to varicose veins. To keep the nerves soft, pregnant women are advised to listen to music and to avoid excesses in eating, drinking, work, and sexual practices. They are also encouraged to avoid those in the community who are believed to have the evil eye, or the ability to worsen wounds.

V

Psychological Conflicts of Mexican-Americans: The Less Severe Disorders

THE ASSISTANCE OF THE CURANDERO is sought for psychiatric disorders of a great range of severity. This chapter focuses on what may be considered the less severe disorders. In contrast to the severe disorders of known etiology, such as the organic syndromes, symptomatic psychoses, and the functional psychoses whose etiology is yet to be determined, these less severe disorders do not develop *de novo*. They arise in part from a matrix of pre-existing psychological conflicts, which are in some measure conditioned by a variety of social, familial, and cultural experiences. In many instances, these patterns are even manifested subclinically in certain characteristic styles of living and relating. An attempt was therefore made to obtain data on the "psychology" of the Mexican-American slum dwellers by way of better understanding the subclinical and clinical problems encountered by the curandero.

We did not attempt to elaborate on all conflicts found among

Mexican-Americans, but only on those salient ones that bore a relationship to the kinds of problems most often encountered by the curandero. Often, a delineation of unconscious tendencies or traits and conflicts tends to carry a derogatory connotation and when lifted from context is interpreted as criticism and condemnation of an entire group of people. This has not been my intention. The traits outlined herein and the conflicts generated by conflicting sets of traits are universal ones. What is important, however, is the particular patterning of these traits and their relationship to the psychiatric disorders. As Devereux has suggested:

> Each society or culture permits certain impulses, fantasies and the like to become and to remain conscious, while requiring others to be repressed. (Devereux, 1956, p. 6)

For this reason, the members of a given culture are likely to have repressed the same things and thereby to have certain unconscious conflicts in common. Devereux has written:

> The same defense mechanisms are present in the normal and in the abnormal personality, as well as in members of various cultures. The normal differs from the abnormal and the Eskimo differs from the Bedouin, not in terms of the presence or absence of certain defense mechanisms, but in terms of the presence or absence of the patterning of all defenses, and in terms of the relative degree of importance which culture "assigns" to the various defense mechanisms. This "assigning" of importance is not a deliberate act, but simply a more or less inevitable by-product of the prevailing cultural atmosphere. (Devereux, 1956, p. 22)

This accounts for the fact that the psychodynamic mechanisms, or the patterning of behavior and defenses, varies from culture to culture which, in turn, is reflected in patterns of psychiatric illnesses. What is of special interest to us is the relationship of these typical conflicts and patterned defenses to the psychiatric disorders recognized by the folk system of psychiatry. Only by looking closely at types of conflicts and types of disorders generated in the Mexican-American slum, are we able to understand the rational basis of the folk theory and the value of the folk therapy. As we shall see, the psychiatry of curanderismo is meaningfully related to the problems that occur in this culture.

Psychological conflicts may be seen as beginning from the time of birth. The birth of a child is a significant event for Mexican-Americans and every woman is expected to have children. Indeed, if a married woman does not have any, family councils are held, special prayers are offered, and home remedies or some form of treatment are attempted. A mother and newborn baby are very much indulged. The mother is cared for by everyone, while babies are immediately picked up and comforted when they cry. Since such efforts represent a shift of ordinary routines, much concern is focused on the psychological impact on the family of the new arrival and on the effect of the mother on the child. As one informant said:

> They feel that it is the baby that needs all the attention and they try to prepare the older children to act on their own and to follow an older child. When this happens the older child may get cranky; it's very common for the older child to get sad when a new child is born. People try to prevent it by trying to divide their care among the children. You take the older child into your confidence, let him hold the baby in his arms and let him be around you when you are taking care of the baby, instead of shooing him away.

Paralleling the awareness of the child's impact on the family is the awareness of the mother's effect on the child. While a wet nurse may be used at first, since the mother's colostrum is not thought to be good, mother's milk is believed to be very important for the child, and breast feeding is encouraged. Great emphasis is also placed on the mother's emotional state during pregnancy and nursing. An angry mother is believed to have angry children; a nervous mother, nervous children. Weaning is done gradually at the end of the second year. The recent adoption of bottle feeding and early, drastic weaning by some working mothers in San Antonio is criticized by many as being both inadequate and traumatic. Most are critical of the Anglo stress on graded frustration to build character. Child-training is geared not to future but to present adjustment and the helplessness of children is not a source of parental distress.

The young mother is expected to seek the assistance of grand-parents and godparents who are obligated to share their experience with her. This tradition sometimes creates tensions between genera-tions since the young mother must often allow grandparents to direct the child care. Some mothers may come to view their children as competitors for attention. Others may welcome this help, which may satisfy their dependency needs, albeit at the price of a dampened independence.

Despite the official joyous welcome accorded pregnancy and childbirth, there is actually ambivalence of attitude. Infants are often left to the care of female relatives whenever their mothers choose to pursue other interests. Such rejection is more radical with the birth of another child. Children "know nothing" and must be silent on command. The ambivalence toward children is seen in the infrequent use made of child-care facilities despite the high incid-ence of child mortality, the frequent giving away of children, and the often brutal treatment of children—all of which are remarkable in a culture which idealizes motherhood and childhood.

Children are toilet-trained after two or two and a half years, during which period they are treated as little adults. They are expected to be seen and not heard, but are permitted to attend adult functions as integral parts of the family. They cease to be the center of family interest and rarely are viewed as potential vehicles of social mobility for the family. Pride in, and loyalty to, family, and duty to God are stressed in their training, as are the virtues of good conduct, shame, and modesty. In contrast, competitiveness, ambi-tion, and individual achievement are discouraged. Excessive expression of emotion, as in temper tantrums, is felt to be unhealthy and active efforts are always taken to indulge children to avoid their having temper tantrums. If they do have them, they are either disciplined or ignored, rarely coddled.

Thus, when the child is able to walk and talk, training becomes coercive and constrictive. Obedience, compliance, and silence are rewarded, while activity, mobility, curiosity, and talkativeness are actively discouraged. During this stage, which Erikson has called the stage of "autonomy," autonomous will and autonomous activity are prohibited (Erikson, 1950). During the next stage ("initiative"—Erikson), curiosity and aggressiveness are discouraged. Repeated frightening tales of *brujas,* ghosts, and the devil are told and physical punishment is administered to keep the child in line. Discipline often takes the form of teasing and ridicule, and children learn to avoid being shamed by inhibiting their behavior. While discipline and child-rearing are the domain of the mother, the father is the final arbiter in all matters. Discipline through threat is less common and children are given little chance to experience "getting away with something." Recourse to the commands of Catholicism is common and children early learn the importance of doing God's wishes so as not to go to hell. The child is thus taught simultaneously to project his aggressions onto the devil and others (*bruja,* people) and to develop institutionalized fears and institutionalized motives for adopting a passive-dependent attitude. As we shall see, these built-in tendencies take on great significance in the folklore of psychological difficulties, many of which are believed to be caused by these same mythical entities which are used to keep children in line. Furthermore, as we shall see, one of the cornerstones of the folk therapy is the opportunity it affords for relinquishing, if only temporarily, many of these early learned inhibitions. Since the family is primarily authoritarian and patriarchal, it is not uncommon for the mother to side with the child and protect him from the father, a pattern which may be related to the later expectation of unqualified support from the Virgin Mary and the Virgin of Guadalupe during sickness. This expectation is heavily reinforced by the curandero's reliance on these religious figures in his ritualistic treatments.

Through the interweaving of strict discipline and the alliance formed between mother and child, many learn to avoid punishment through deception, a pattern which a protective mother may teach her children when she assists them in avoiding the wrath of their father. At times the pattern of deception is even more widespread in family groups, and seems directly related to the extent of parental deceptions. Children may be punished irrespective of their denials. This leads to an accentuation of cautiousness in interpersonal relationships with an associated tendency to disguise feelings from others, a pattern of behavior which is idealized by Mexican-Americans. That such deceptions lead to guilt feelings is a well-documented clinical fact and undoubtedly relates to the relief of anxiety from confession to an authority figure, another cornerstone of the curandero's therapy. Indeed, it is likely that almost everyone in this culture suffers from conflicts created by habitually trying to avoid intimacy through partial deceptions. Deception, in bringing to the fore an individual's basic dependency needs and inclinations to submit, increases his burden of resentment, hostility, and guilt.

Relations between boys and girls assume a formal pattern at the age of five or six, when sex-related behavior patterns are introduced. Usually boys are more severely punished as well as more indulged, although all children are expected to be obedient, silent, and loyal. Boys are expected to be courageous—not in the sense of aggressiveness, curiosity, and work, but in the sense of physical strength and endurance of physical pain. When not attending school, boys and girls start working with parents of the same sex around age seven. At this stage of development, when the process of identification with parents takes place, the child is more likely to incorporate a world view shaped by agricultural and religious traditions that are authoritarian, stable, and unchanging than he is to adopt one affected by American values. Stereotyped relations with God and the family constitute the major part of his learning. The dogmatic interpretation and practice of Catholicism, with its fatalistic attribution of all power and will to one supreme force, also play a significant role in the establishment and maintenance of this stable world. In this setting, religion and tradition provide a faith for the child that may not be provided adequately by the human and natural environment. However, this faith reinforces the family experience and encourages the acceptance of helplessness and of fatalistic, passive-dependent expectations. At the same time, prohibition of self-expression and aggressiveness leads to an accumulation of aggression which can only find its expression in culturally sanctioned areas. To summarize, it appears likely that passivity, the accumulation of drives, and ever-increasing social need and demand for powerful mastery of one's own drives become essential areas of conflict with the Mexican's ego.

areas of Pso conflict

In Mexico, the severe discipline, coupled with the emphasis on formality, produces strong aggressive drives, the expression of which are encouraged through sanctioned outlets. In Mexican-American culture, by contrast, there are fewer sanctioned outlets and, as a result, instinctual needs, particularly aggressive drives which are not expressed or channeled, create more conflicts for people. To some extent, the formality that makes for these strong aggressive drives also keeps them in check. Thus, there are strict rules governing relationships with relatives, and specific behavior patterns and linguistic forms appropriate to different categories of kin have to be learned. Siblings are expected to be affectionate and cooperative with each other and overt competition and aggression are vigorously discouraged. Concern for family functions is stressed. Older girls assist in caring for younger children and older boys serve as household heads in the absence of the father. Brothers are expected to protect and to defend the honor of their sisters; younger children, to respect the older children. The father maintains authority through tradition and sometimes by force, but mostly by being somewhat aloof, by criticizing unacceptable acts, by withholding praise for acceptable acts, and by keeping to himself feelings of love, respect, and concern.

Father

The tendency to remain distant and to inhibit the expression of positive feelings is often a source of tension between the father and children. This tension is particularly evident in urban areas where there are few shared activities such as one finds in rural agrarian situations. While formal rules and traditional obligations help to keep the tension in check, overt conflicts often occur during adolescence, particularly regarding expressions of independence. Because of verbal or physical suppression, these conflicts often take the form of anti-social behavior. Parental concerns focus on conformity and obedience rather than on individual achievement and activities, and are another source of conflict, especially when children are educated in America and are relatively more successful than their parents.

The mother's relationship to her sons, although characterized by much love and concern, is not a reciprocal one since close identification with women is frowned upon. Some mothers maintain their relationship through exaggerated protectiveness, permissiveness, and excessive claims of martyrdom which tend to intensify the loyalties of their children to them. As part of their covert alliance with their children against the authoritarian head of the family, mothers often undermine their husbands by talking about acts they have committed. While this may strengthen their own position in the home it may encourage a loss of self-esteem, a sense of self-disrespect, and ambivalence about masculine identification in male children, and a lack of confidence in men and future husbands in female children. Identification with the father does, however, satisfy various passive and aggressive needs in sons and does promote a readier acceptance of the traditional culture. It is made easier by the son's observations of his mother's attitude toward men, from which boys learn that women cannot be trusted.

The narcissistic attitude of Mexican mothers toward their infants, coupled with their tendency to identify with their children as sibling rivals, leads them to over-indulge and infantilize their children, which ultimately prevents successful differentiation of ego and id, and critically affects the child's psychosexual and psychosocial development. This early traumatization and restriction of potential psychic maturational capacities is compounded by abrupt displacement by younger rivals and observations of hostile expressions by adults. For males, additional strain is later introduced by the absence of an adequate masculine object of identification. Females, by contrast, have better opportunities for identification

55

with maternal figures. Subsequent trauma during later stages of socialization result in further oral fixations and all psychosexual phases are fused with orality in one way or another. Experiences with discrimination may also be seen as contributing to the perpetuation of psychologically undesirable residues of these traumatic socialization experiences.

Customary belief to the contrary, the female appears to be the strong figure in the household and her role is more consistent than that of the male. This finding is consistent with the observations made of other acculturating groups. Studying the Ojibwa, Caudill found that women are better able to make satisfactory adjustments to conditions of acculturation than are men. (Caudill, 1949) This conclusion is particularly so since the early identifications of children in all societies are with mothering figures. The male child must go further and identify with male figures. In Mexican-American culture the child inevitably retains bisexual identification partly because of faulty id-ego differentiation and partly because of the personal, familial, and societal weakness of the father.

Difficulties in forming adequate male identity show up in the persistence and accentuation of patterns of drunkenness and promiscuity. While Mexican village society formalizes certain outlets for masculine assertion, these are much less available in San Antonio. The nature of the Mexican personality structure has its basis in the early abandonment of and failure to relate to infants by the narcissistic mother, and subsequent rejection by the father. The typical present-day Mexican-American searches for an adequate mother-infant relationship in all his activities. Even the seeking for a father figure may constitute a search for the mother.

Hallowell and Caudill found that major personality characteristics persist over time despite influences of acculturation, and Boyer has suggested that this finding is true, even though deculturation and inability or refusal to accept acculturation prevail, as in cases in which negative identity develops among the Mexican-Americans. (Hallowell, 1936; Boyer, R.M., 1962) The typical personality structure of the Mexican is similar to that observed in the

Mexican-American. But the Mexican-American has not had the stable and internally flexible social structure of the Mexican village, which provided means by which the conditions of abnormality stimulated and promoted by socialization processes could be consistently sanctioned and formalized, thus making individual functioning less conflictual than in America today.

A major source of stress in the Mexican and Mexican-American family is the son's conflict between parental domination and traditional respect and obedience. (Farris, 1963; Ramirez, 1957) The urge for independence is further complicated by guilt of "hurting" the loving mother and fear of the punitive father. Mexican and Mexican-American males thus encounter problems of submission, conflict, and rebellion in the area of authority; preoccupation and anxiety regarding sexual potency; conflict and ambivalence regarding the expression of feelings; and conflicts of overcoming dependency on over-protective mothers. As Rogelio Diaz-Guerrero has noted, males are caught in a compulsive asking for forgiveness from the same symbol (mother) they must betray if they are to be masculine. It is only because a good number succeed in keeping each role distinct and separate through clear discrimination of the places and situations suitable for each, that no more serious mental disturbances appear. (Diaz-Guerrero, 1955)

Girls encounter just as complex but different problems in adhering to the unrealistic standards set for them. The result is the development of certain characteristic feminine traits, most notably self-belittlement and depressive trends. In typical families with authoritarian fathers, girls learn both tolerance for frustration and techniques for dealing with frustration from their mothers. The jealousy of the Mexican-American male relates not only to fear of feminine rejection and masculine insecurity, but also in part to the wife's ability to arouse her husband's jealousy in order to maintain her own security.*

* Certain of these patterns are changing in the urban areas. Since the regulation of behavior in terms of shame, pride, and modesty depends on the presence of large primary groups, the Mexican in San Antonio is less

Because of the rigid sex differentiation in this culture, identification with the opposite sex parent must be repressed. Aggressiveness in a woman is held as proof that she is a "bad woman" or "witch" and is such an ego-alien trait that anyone expressing it is likely to feel herself to be *embrujada*.

Courtesy, formality, and respect toward parents is extended to relationships with others, and the ideal man and woman are paragons of self-control. Women especially are careful to avoid spontaneous expressions of friendliness which might be misinterpreted as flirtations or promiscuity, and men avoid gossiping for fear of being labeled "old women." As one woman said:

> Some men can't stand women to gossip. My husband can't stand another woman to be in the house when he comes home, when he's tired and disgusted with the day's work and he don't feel like having anybody there. Gossip they don't like—they claim that's what starts a fight with menfolks. Gossip will lead to the men's fighting—it does sometimes. I seen it in real life in my husband. First, it starts with the kids, and the wives get into it, and the first thing you know, the husbands are involved.

This idealized pattern of noninvolvement is reinforced and no doubt contributes to beliefs about the evil eye. Since emotions are dangerous and have a power of their own, they are guarded against. Even smiling at a pretty child may, it is believed, bring about *mal ojo*. Excessive emotionality and loss of self-control are component parts of many folk illnesses. The premium placed on self-control is reinforced by the above discussed customs relating to social formality and courtesies which structure interpersonal relationships among everyone but children and old people (and those in the sick role). Individuals are judged by their conformity to these social norms. Individuals select close friends cautiously, as too much familiarity is believed to be potentially dangerous. Detachment from

---

constrained than when in Mexico and is thus more likely to express his inner conflicts. This can be seen in greater sexual license and more open expression of aggression—among both men and women.

others provides some security, however, since by not sharing one's feelings or ambitions one avoids the envy of others. In this sense, humility and self-restraint are protective mechanisms as well as desirable traits.

Personal fear of "losing control" finds its counterpart in the rationalized belief that man does not control his own destiny. Uncertainty about other people and about life in general extends even to marital partners. Suspiciousness and jealousy of one's wife is a commonly reported sentiment. It relates both to experiences in trusting others and to specific sexual patterns and attitudes such as the tacit approval of Don Juanism in men and the strict controls placed over women, who simultaneously are over-idealized.

Spontaneous emotional expression is discouraged except in certain specified situations or in certain specified ways. In the case of aggression, this may be through gossip, sorcery, or ridicule, fear of which serves to maintain the status quo, as does the belief that excessive anger may lead to illness. The idealized male or *"macho"* does not fight back immediately when challenged or insulted, but waits for a more propitious time for retaliation or resorts to sorcery. When aggression is expressed directly it is usually violent and brutal and associated with alcohol. This fact suggests the difficulty for Mexican-Americans of expressing anger in a controlled way. Extreme violence and even murder are tacitly accepted when they involve sexual jealousy and infidelity.

Sex is believed to be a necessary evil that women must accept, and an uncontrollable, excessive, "animal" instinct for men. Mutual sexual satisfaction in marriage is not sought and, indeed, a wife's enjoyment of sexual relations is often considered a justifiable cause for suspicion of infidelity. Marriages are made in accordance with God's will, not for self-fulfillment, mutual sexual satisfaction, or the joys of intimacy. Sexual play between husband and wife is taboo. The sexual exploits of men occur with unrespectable women or prostitutes, never with wives.

Young girls early learn to fear, distrust, and tolerate men. The ideal wife is submissive, faithful, and obedient. A woman who is beaten into submission may receive little sympathy from others. While the husband is ostensibly responsible for major family decisions and for economic support, and women are considered less reliable and trustworthy, the wife usually has much authority in the home. Men must guard against their wives breaking away from the restraints of tradition because of their weaker wills and basically unstable nature. Women view men as unreliable but are tolerant of their infidelities. The increased freedom of women in urban areas in the United States and the diminution of the extended family have intensified conflicts in this area.

According to Lewis, the domination of a man by his wife in Mexico suggests to all that she must have doctored his food and rendered him stupid and foolish. (Lewis, 1963) Such a belief relates to the fact that feminine domination is not sanctioned and is a source of anxiety. A domineering or independent woman thus may be considered a witch or a consort of the devil. Even if a young mother resents an interefering mother-in-law, she may be accused of a relationship with the devil. The daughter-in-law may also be blamed for bewitching her husband, if the mother-in-law claims alienation of affection by an independent son.

As are social relations, sexual relations are expected to be characterized by male initiative and feminine passivity. Women are expected to have less sexual desire than men. When they show interest in sex they are suspected of promiscuity. When they are promiscuous they are thought to be suffering from "furor" due to an oversized clitoris or bewitchment. If a wife is frigid it is not looked upon as a bad thing, since a husband may be secure in knowledge that she will be unlikely to seek adulterous liaisons. In addition, wives' characteristic disinterest may be less emotionally challenging for the men, who appear to have problems in fusing tender and sexual feelings. This double standard, whereby sexual relations are considered all right for men and all wrong for women, supports the kinds of relations that characteristically develop in this culture.

The emphasis on formality and the suppression of feelings relates not only to negative feelings, but also to such positive feelings as love, affection, and tenderness. These are not usually expressed in a spontaneous way, but in certain patterned or institutionalized ways such as poetry and song, where they are likely to be idealized.

These inhibitions derive from the early learning experiences in the family, described above. The mother who turns to her sons for emotional gratification may by her over-protectiveness and over-solicitude foster much anxiety, resentment, and hostility toward women. That this is generally so is supported by the widespread belief in powerful witches and evil women who bewitch men into marriage through love philtres or magic. Sexual activity with a mother figure such as the good wife, which arouses Oedipal conflicts, is avoided. While sexual activity per se is not threatening and is readily sought after, the avoidance of a spouse derives in part from the over-idealization of women and the inability to fuse love and sex. Mexican-American women generally accept the view that they should not enjoy sexuality, and in this way complement their needs.

These Oedipal patterns appear also in the high value placed on such traits as recklessness, resoluteness, and self-assurance, which are best exemplified in the idealized male, or *macho*. The emphasis on masculine pride, courage, and self-control relates to castration fears generated in the authoritarian family setting. The institutionalization of certain expected reactions to slights and ridicule of masculinity affirms the widespread presence of these fears. This is supported by psychoanalytic theory, which has shown that pride and courage, as well as bashfulness and timidity (which are the corresponding desirable traits admired in women) are clearly related to conflicts of the castration complex.

Another significant emotional complex in this culture relates to marked ambivalence in interpersonal relationships and conflicts over the ability to love. This complex relates in part to the fact that individuals enter marriage with many unfulfilled dependency needs and with inadequate preparation for responsibility. These problems are reflected in jealous attitudes and expressions in interpersonal relations and in the institutionalization of certain beliefs and formalized responses to jealousy. According to Fenichel, the mixture of depression, aggressiveness, and envy with which a jealous person reacts to loss of love is more intense in personalities for whom this loss means a decrease in their self-esteem, as well as in those who have early experienced this loss of love. (Fenichel, 1945) Certainly for the Mexican male, the infidelity of his wife or the suspicion of such is a severe blow to his position in the community and to his own self concept but it is even more upsetting because it reactivates the earlier experienced castration anxiety and feelings of rejection. That these anxieties are widespread is suggested by the fact that control against possible misconduct on the part of wives is institutionalized, as in the acceptable prohibition that married women should not gossip with neighbors.

The prevalence of jealousy relates also to the fact that the close affectional ties that children, especially boys, establish with their mothers are never completely certain, stable, or satisfactory because of the resentment and fear of their fathers that is simultaneously induced. In addition, because of the minimum of parental mutuality, and the child's observations of his mother's deception of the father and her subtle demeaning of him, he is likely to anticipate the same from a wife. Jealousy also arises, according to psychoanalytic theory, wherever a necessity to repress impulses toward unfaithfulness and homosexuality meet with the intolerance of loss of love. All these factors are also widespread in this culture. The strong pressure on men to betray their wives because of the *machismo* complex is likely to increase men's tendencies to project their own wishes onto their wives, a process which further leads to widespread social restrictions on women.

The clear-cut role definitions of men and women, husbands and wives, parents and children maintain a certain stability in the face of these unresolved conflicts. Conflicts that cannot be resolved by full adoption of specific age and sex roles may be manifested in projections of unconscious motives—such as male jealousy or feminine acceptance of promiscuity among men, which perhaps indirectly satisfies their own heterosexual longings.

An inclination to be suggestive, to react to minimal stimuli with irrational emotional outbreaks, to stress the dramatic and the histrionic, and even, in children, to accept mendacity (traits frequently attributed to Mexican-Americans) are, according to Fenichel, expressions of an individual's readiness to reactivate infantile types of object relationships. These traits are found among Mexican-Americans and clearly relate to difficulties in escaping from early patterns developed in relation to controlling indulgent mothers and suppressive fathers.

While jealousy seems common among men, a strong masochistic trend appears pronounced among women. Relating to the strong prohibitions surrounding feminine sexuality is the presumed disinterest in sexual activity among Mexican women. This is a form of frigidity which reflects anxiety about sexual expression. Such anxiety follows from identification of the husband with the father, from fear of losing control, and from the value placed on masochistic traits in women. Masochism may serve protective purposes. It may represent a reunion with a protective omnipotent power, a demonstration of helplessness, and an appeal to the mercy of threatening figures in the environment. By exhibiting her misery, the Mexican woman may express hostility indirectly and at the same time, may derive benefits from those around her, and able to control interpersonal situations. Quiet rebellion against a restrictive upbringing and efforts at ingratiation are the source motives of such behavior. Accepting the martyr role both as a daughter and as a wife enables the Mexican woman to demonstrate that she is not deserving of punishment. By suffering, a woman unconsciously gains protection and relief and also makes others feel guilty.

Another prominent pattern and source of conflict is the persistence of dependency behavior into adulthood. Because the Mexican-American mother acts as a nursing mother even past the early childhood of her children, the Mexican-American child is forever expecting to have his dependency needs gratified by the environment. The nursing mother is at the same time a dependent person herself. By her generosity she demands the same care in return, so that interpersonal relationships bring much mutual satisfaction of dependency needs. The immature nature of this mutuality and generosity is suggested by the fact that while oral satisfaction leads to self-assurance and optimism, frustration leads to vengefulness coupled with continuous demanding and a basically dependent attitude toward the universe. Furthermore, the Mexican-American is prone to leave things up to God, is suspicious and reticent about trusting people, and is readily willing to seek revenge if his dependency needs are challenged.

Because children are rewarded on the basis of their adherence to certain fixed standards of behavior, they are inclined to be dependent upon others for the maintenance of their self-esteem. While all children need the support and approval of others, especially parents, for the satisfaction of their dependency needs and the development of self-esteem, the Mexican child's experience would appear to be one where other sources of self-esteem are not encouraged. That is to say, the child is not encouraged, as are American children, to develop independent patterns of activity which will bring satisfaction to him independent of others. Because of the system of rewards and punishments, the child remains forever dependent upon others for his feelings of self-esteem. This system is reinforced by the necessity to conform to external rules. This system also derives from the extended family groupings and the emphasis upon the family rather than upon the individual. Other sources of security and support which reinforce dependent tendencies include the belief in magic and miracles and the patron system, whereby wealthy landowners are expected to act as benefactors toward the less fortunate.

Conflict over dependency needs are accentuated by the fact that individuals are permitted to express dependency needs consciously only when they are sick, which as we shall see, is of great significance in the type of therapy used by the curandero. Conflict is also seen in the fluctuations from extreme suspiciousness and avoidance of others to excessive generosity and openness and in the idealization of the *macho* and the *muy mujera,* who show no dependent traits. Such idealized types exhibit counter-phobic and compensatory mechanisms to the fear of castration and loss of dependency supports.

Conflicts over dependency are particularly accentuated in those who have renounced their families and become acculturated to the American way of life. Such people are called *agringados* and are usually social climbers, prostitutes, drunkards, and others who have broken with Mexican traditions. It is believed that members of specific racial-ethnic groups, such as Mexicans conceive *La Raza,* are born with certain predetermined racial characteristics. By trying to become something he is not, an individual loses his inborn sources of strength, incurs the wrath of God, and becomes subject to the dangers of overwhelming ambition. Such individuals are likely to become sick furthermore, because they are not *contentado,* or satisfied.

Madsen found a high proportion of problem drinkers among a group of *agringados* or *inglesados* in South Texas (Madsen, 1964b) Because of increased economic opportunities in Anglo society, particularly since World War II, more and more Mexican-Americans have acquired Anglo values. At the same time, they adhere to customs maintaining their cultural identity. The adoption of two sets of conflicting values creates problems for many. Thus, because of the emphasis on parental respect, most young Mexican-Americans suppress outward manifestations of Anglo values in the presence of elders. Those like the *agringados,* who reject Mexican customs in favor of Anglo customs, are often rejected and ridiculed not only by Mexicans, but also by Anglos as well. Of the various escapes from value conflict, such as moving elsewhere, over-identification with Mexican values, antisocial behavior, and persistent efforts at acculturation, Madsen found the last to be associated with alcoholism among the Mexican-Americans of South Texas. The individual who seeks self-advancement through personal efforts and rejects the Mexican emphasis on the family and the subordination of the individual to the will of the father, may attempt to resolve these incompatible orientations through excessive drinking, which in both groups is identified with masculine assertion (although a Mexican must be able to back up anything he says while drinking, must be able to hold his liquor, and must not appear drunk before his parents). In Mexican culture there is a strong association among intoxicating beverages, manliness, and sociability. With this background the Mexican-American may fail to comprehend the ambivalent Anglo-American attitude toward drinking, whereby his excessive indulgence will lead to rejection. Because of rejection by his family an *agringado* may drink excessively, expecting Anglo acceptance, without recognizing that he may also be rejected by the Anglos for this. The drinking *agringado*, by exclusion from Mexican-American society, is relieved of many of the social restraints on excess. When he discovers he is rejected by Anglos as well, he may blame his plight on witchcraft or punishment by God for his failure to be a good son—a maneuver which may, as Madsen has so clearly shown, lead to his reintegration into the Mexican-American group.

The attitude toward *agringados* was expressed by one person as follows:

> These are people who disinherit themselves from the family. Well, if the father was a guy like my daddy was, he would seal you off once and for all. Well, if he thought he wasn't good enough that he was sacrificing and working all the time, if it wasn't good enough for them, the sons and daughters would just say "go your way." The parents don't feel guilty usually. It is the sons and daughters who feel guilty. Sometimes the son and daughter get homesick ; sometimes the family won't accept them back. Usually they get sick at that time from *tristeza*, unhappiness. Then they go to a curandero for treatment, talk out their troubles. Curandero will tell them to rejoin their family.

The conflicts emerging from these patterns of family life and interpersonal behavior are intensified by adherence to a number of important values (expressing the emotionally charged preferences, attitudes, and goals of the group) which are at variance with each other and with certain American values. To understand the general nature of these values, it is important to remember that Mexican-American culture derives from a rural folk background that was little influenced by the Renaissance, Reformation, or Industrial Revolution. In this self-contained, static, agrarian society, the development of marketable skills and motivations for social mobility were unnecessary and as such not valued. More important, as Saunders has shown, were a high regard for authority, adherence to tradition, a philosophy of acceptance and resignation, and a sacred orientation. Americans, on the other hand, value achievement and success, activity and work, a pragmatic moral orientation, humanitarianism (as opposed to authoritarianism), efficiency and practicality (as opposed to form, pomp, role-playing), material comfort (as opposed to a willingness to put up with the hardships of life), equality of opportunity (as opposed to the patron system), freedom (as opposed to the bondage of children to parents), external conformity, science (as opposed to magic), secular rationality (as opposed to traditionalism), democracy, nationalism, patriotism, and individual personality (as opposed to a group-centered orientation). In a rural, agrarian society the present was the focus of interest rather than the future. Present obligations and social relationships were more important than personal goals, and traditional ways were more important than new ways. As Saunders has written:

> There being no jobs, no first of the month bills, no pressure toward competition, no formal organizations, no particular value placed on preciseness of any kind, few clocks, and no resources or skills with which more could readily be constructed, there was no pressure to develop any particular concern with the time. (Saunders, 1954, p. 120)

Related to this present-time orientation is the relative lack of emphasis on efficiency, adaptability, technological innovation, modernity, and expediency, which are all highly valued in American society. For the Mexican, work is not a virtue and a man's job is considered neither his major source of prestige in the community nor the means of identifying him. The Mexican accepts the world as God made it and since he does not feel responsible for his own future, he does not actively change it. Salvation in the hereafter comes to those with faith in God and the Trinity.

Such fatalism pervades many aspects of Mexican-American as well as Latin American culture and is symbolized, according to Gillin, by the bullfight:

> The matador pits all his skill against the bull, which is Death incarnate. But he does it with fitness, imperturbability, and with grace. If he is successful, Man has once more defied and conquered Death—for the time being . . . . The sense of fatalism may be manifested in the seemingly fanatical defiance of danger by soldiers and revolutionary mobs, in an apparent willingness to endure hardships disproportionate to the goal at hand and to take risks beyond all rationality. The elaborate cult of death, funerals, and graveyards is a further expression of the value attached to fatalism. (Gillin, 1960, p. 45-46)

This fatalism, coupled with guilt, fear of the dead, and limited emotional expression, can be seen in attitudes toward and beliefs about the dead. For the Mexican, life and death are not separate and distinct but are phases of the same cosmic cycle. It is a common belief that after death, a man's soul may live on in the form of a spirit or ghost. Survivors attempt to placate the dead by speaking only good things of them and praying to them, hoping to prevent their return. At funerals, weeping is discouraged and memories repressed. It is believed that the bereaved spouse is in great danger of being pulled to join the dead one if he or she grieves excessively, or if the dead spouse is jealous.

Catholicism, according to Paz, modified the Aztec's concept of sacrifice and introduced the idea of individual rather than collective salvation. (Paz, 1961) For the Aztec, the sacrifice rejuvenated the cosmos or the universe, not the individual. In the Catholic view it is the individual who counts. It is the world, not the man, which is condemned and redemption is a personal task. At the same time, death is still only a transition between life on this earth and life in the other world.

As a result of this view, the Mexican has, according to Paz, an indifferent attitude toward death and is not angry, frightened, and confused by it. He is indifferent to death because he is indifferent to life. Life, according to Paz, has caused the Mexican to be fearless of death. It is believed that death is natural and at times desirable. Life is of less value as an abstract entity.

Death has been made into something of a cult, according to Paz, and is present in fiestas, games, thoughts. Death is, for some, a violent explosion of repressed emotions and angers. Death, too, reminds the Mexicans of his own view of life for, as Paz has written: "Death strips life of all its vanities and pretensions and converts it into what it really is, a few neat bones and a dreadful grimance." (Paz, 1961, p. 58)

The Mexican often decorates his house with death's heads and eats bread in the shape of bones on the Day of the Dead, a national holiday. Bread and cookies in animal or human shapes are prepared, special candles are sold, and children are given "Jack-in-the-boxes" from out of which pop skeletons. This is the day for picnicing at cemeteries and planting flowers at the graves. On this day the dead return to share in the festivities, and special dishes are set aside for them. All Saints' Day follows a similar pattern but honors the *angelitos*.

In Catholic families a rosary is said for nine nights following death to ensure the departure of the soul to heaven. Wakes are social events, those for children being particularly gay in keeping with the Catholic belief that children are free from sin and go to heaven as *angelitos*. Some believe if the *angelitos* have been well treated, they will intercede for those on earth, since because of their purity, their influence in heaven is great.

The belief that the road to the next world is a difficult one is still held. It is thought that the dead often meet troublesome animals, thorns, and so on. Many also believe that the dead must cross a river and that a little dog swims them across. On the other side of the river is a man who points the way. They next come to a gate, which is purgatory. The dead are conscious of what is going on until they enter a church in purgatory and receive last rites, after which they continue, but forget those left behind. Funerals, which unite the family and community and provide a supportive experience for the bereaved, render respect to the dead soul and ensure its passage to heaven, thereby protecting the living from the potential harm of a remaining spirit.

The fatalism manifested in relation to illness and death has been bolstered by the Catholic Church, which has encouraged a group rather than individualist orientation. The Puritan emphasis, by contrast, was on individual character, and the Puritan believed he could change his circumstances by effort. Those who failed, failed from moral feelings and were to be condemned. The Puritan spirit found its expression in the middle and commercial classes but such a spirit never developed in Mexico. As Tawney has written:

> The moral self-sufficiency of the Puritan nerved his will, but it corroded his sense of social solidarity . . . . . A spiritual aristocrat who sacrificed fraternity to liberty, he drew from his idealization of personal responsibility a theory of individual rights which secularized and generalized was to be among the most potent explosives that the world has known. (Tawney, 1926, p. 229-230)

Mexican-Americans are inclined to judge people not by their achievements but in terms of particularistic criteria, such as how they get on with their families and children and whether they are good sons, fathers, husbands, and believers in the Church's doctrines. If an individual follows religious precepts he is praised and rewarded, but if he tries to change his lot or God's will, he is criticized. Mexican-Americans are more concerned with a man's character and his sense of pride than they are with his objective success. As one person interviewed said:

> Mexicans are more interested in the kind of character a person has than in the amount of money he has. They respect a man more

who respects his family than any man in the world. A Mexican man would like to be honest, work hard, and do their day's work by doing an honest day's work. They like to work in the day and then enjoy and go out like anybody else, have a few beers sometimes, they can't do it all the time. In America, children are raised differently. My Daddy used to say, "When you go out and work, if you make $5.00 you don't spend all $5.00—you would be like the fox, he'd spend $2.00 and save $3.00 for a rainy day." You've got to be wise, not by working every day, gotta be careful how you spend your money, otherwise brother, you are in for it. Then, there's some—I don't know why, they are not raised right, they just throw everything out, just like a lost week. I'll tell you what is wrong in Mexico, they claim people don't get much pay. Often, the poor people gotta work for little pay for the people that have got money. I imagine it is the same thing all over the world. They try to raise the kids, show them religion, show them pride.

The emphasis on the group and particularistic criteria leads to a great sensitivity regarding individuality which takes a different form among Mexican-Americans than among Anglos. As the Spanish writer Iturriaga has written:

> The Mexican is not gregarious, but individualistic, and as a consequence he often lacks the spirit of collaboration. His unsociability and asperity unfit him to live with others without friction or to work creatively as a member of a team. (Iturriaga, 1951, p. 233)

Related to the high value placed on individuality in a situation where group values are emphasized are certain idealized character types. Thus, the *machismo* displays sexual prowess, a zest for action, daring, and self-confidence, qualities least likely to be developed in the kind of family and social system we have described.

As a safeguard against treading on the sensitiveness of an individual's dignity, interpersonal relations are often highly formalized and individuals tend to remain distant from strangers, only establishing intimate relationships with long-time acquaintances. American customs are sometimes difficult for Mexican-Americans to understand. For example, in work situations, they expect greater personal contact with employers, as had been true in Mexico for patrons and god-parents, who supported the less fortunate in return for allegiance and loyalty. The Mexican-American values interdependence more than independence and is comfortable in an institutionally defined dependency role. People who do not cooperate in such reciprocal relationships are strongly criticized as self-interested, egotistical, ambitious, greedy, and envious. Individual expression is controlled by such patterned obligations in both the family and the community. By contrast, notions of unlimited opportunity and an unfixed social and world order predominate in Anglo culture and are strongly related to the notion of equality. Mexicans do not feel that equality is an inalienable right, and individuals do not aspire to be more than they are, to change through individual achievement.

The anxieties of childhood training are joined to the learning of traditional roles and social forms, not to the development of independence, frustration tolerance, or skill at adapting to new situations. Such training prepares the child for a stable pattern of relationships rather than for changing relationship patterns, and he learns to be more restrained than manipulative in his dealings with people and with life.

Indeed, as we have seen, a basic dynamic theme in Mexican culture is the fear of being unrestrained and of losing control of one's feelings. Loss of control is so ego-alien in this culture that it is usually viewed either as a manifestation of illness or as the influence of outside forces. This attitude acts as a sanction against excessive emotionality and violation of norm behavior and, at the same time, provides a set of rationalizations which minimize individual responsibility. Great weight is placed on safeguarding the inner worth, dignity, and value of the individual and on the virtues of self-restraint, self-reliance, and silent suffering.

The defensiveness and reticence of individuals thus has psychological and group origins. Gillin has called this *Dignidad de la persona*, "the inner integrity or worth which every person is supposed to have originally and which he is supposed to guard zealously." Every person is supposed to defend his integrity to the utmost of his ability and a person who submits abjectly is usually regarded as much "lower" than one who merely breaks the laws. Words or actions that are personally insulting are highly explosive and evoke emotional reactions which seem exaggerated and "unrealistic," such as verbal or physical violence, sullen resentment, refusal to cooperate and/or seeking "revenge." At the same time, elaborate patterns of ceremonial politeness, in constant use between all but the closest friends and kinsmen, insulates relationships from such insults. As Gillin has written:

> I should add, however, that I do not regard this matter exactly as "saving face" ; "face" an English idiom refers to "externals". In Latin America, *dignidad* is an "internal" matter, the "external" aspects of which are incidentals. One of the subleties outsiders often have difficulty with is that these ceremonial precautions are not necessary when reference is made to merely clearly understood and commonly recognized social positions. For example, it is no insult to his dignidad to address a waiter or common laborer as *Mozo,* although except in the case of old family retainers and master servant relationships of longstanding, you will get better service if you use certain polite forms. (Gillin, 1955, p. 493)

A good example of formality is the pattern associated with donship, which demonstrates a number of interwoven values. (Edmonson, 1957; Foster, 1953) Respected elders who have either been born to or acquired a significant position are referred to as *don.* According to Romano (1960), donship signifies public recognition of socially defined male authority and independence. To merit the title of *don* an individual must behave in an "educated" manner, and know how to "defend" himself in verbal dueling and from *envidia,* witchcraft, and gossip.

Such individuals are able to reconcile their dependency needs with their fear of rejection and anticipation of undependability on the part of others. As Romano has written:

> In this field of super kin social interaction, the most basic premise which governs behavior holds that the world is fickle

and undependable. Individuals outside the kin group are almost invariably suspect and quite normally a stranger is judged guilty until proven innocent. Thus, the burden of "proof" lies with the non-relative and the stranger. These widely held views largely dictate the solution of malehood's problems. And, with distrust of non-kin commonplace, the solution of such problems as exist, takes on a pattern of avoidance, uninvolvement, and oft times withdrawal from extra-familial or community-wide associations. As regards the withdrawal avoidance pattern characteristic of Frontera male life is completed with retrenchment within the kin group, in most instances in the bilateral extended family. (Romano, 1960, p. 969)

In order to solve the various problems of getting along with one's neighbors, the individual in his early life must learn how to defend himself, and how to play his role in the system of expected courtesies, such as the donship concept. All these, according to Romano, "primarily serve to maintain social distance, both vertically with reference to elders and horizontally with reference to neighbors and strangers." The individual also defends himself by learning how to duel verbally, how to stand up to challenges, how to avoid getting too close to people, particularly those who are younger than himself, how to limit his close friendships to a single confidant, and how to maintain relationships with employers who are, by and large, considered untrustworthy. Essentially then, the individual must learn how to recognize when his *dignidad* is threatened, and how to manfully avoid and withdraw from threatening situations. The same attitudes of untrustworthiness apply to women, who are considered basically unfaithful creatures.

Related to this emphasis on form and *dignidad* is the custom of verbal dueling, whereby individuals attempt to penetrate the mask of silence through insult. The object is to arouse emotional reaction on the part of another who at the same time strives to remain unaffected. As one informant described it:

This is a kind of joking quarrel. They can start joking, but it ends up in a real fight. Both boys and girls are taught to argue this way, like for example my daughter comes home from school and say some of the kids not hit her, but try to make her feel like an "odd ball." Well, I tell her there's more than one way to tell somebody off—all you have to do is keep your mouth shut and keep your ears open and you learn. If anybody is going to make you feel as low as a snake, you can make them twice as low if you know how to back them up. I'm that way, I never let anybody pull me down—you don't just tell 'em off, like they try to make a joke of you—you try telling them something that will really hurt them, fire it right back at them. And I try to teach my daughter that cause, see, I can't be with her all the time, and sometimes she comes home kinda upset, and I tell her that's not the way to take it. If you pay attention to everyone you would be a nervous wreck. As we said, if you can't beat them, you can join them . . . . just keep quiet about it, either keep quiet or you hit them back with something stronger . . . . well, for example, take my case, I was working one time and I was married—that was before I had my last boy, and this guy used to be the boss of all the women. One of those guys, he thinks he's got everything a woman would want, and so, anyway, we was picking carrots and one of them stepped on the carrots and I said to this guy "hey, why don't you watch what you are doing?" And I showed him the carrots, so he turned around and he remarked at me, "don't tell me you don't like 'em big." I knew what he was hinting at. I said, "don't call yourself on the line," that is, "don't call yourself number one class." By that I meant he didn't fit into the category. He wasn't good enough for me. When I said that he went to the rear, and he didn't come back to the front for a long time. He was an old man about fifty, you know, real skinny like. I used to respect him, but from that day, he just looked out because every time he came around, I was ready for him. He was trying to get that old maid next to me to flush, and that girl turned as red as beet, and she said "Did you hear what he said?" I said, "I don't give a hoot what he said." Man, I'm married, and I said, "If he's gonna try and fool around with me, he's gonna get it." I said, "Whenever that ole goat thinks he can play the . . . . Ha!— he's just gonna get it. He just aint worth the dirt I gonna step on. He never did bother me. If it's a young girl, they will flush and feel bad about it, but I am not that way. And the other men were laughing at this old goat.

You are not supposed to show that you are shy because the more you are, the more they are going to try and hit you down, and from there on in, I just stand and stare them in the eye, and this other man was laughing. I said to him, "That will teach you to keep your mouth shut." You hurt them the more by just going up and saying some words than if you pick a fight. Just keep calm and told them off.

Between women sometimes, a younger woman may accuse an older woman of being too old to get a man and the older woman will be accusing younger women of being "hussies." Actually the reason is that people try to get each other mad so they walk out on the job so that there's more money for those who continue to stay on the job.

Some of the men say they can do better with women and some say they can outdrink each other, drink them under the table, or "I can play better pool than you can," "I can do better with the women"—some of them get on that side [women], others of them don't. The real man avoids this: he stands above it. He just figures he's a man and nobody's going to know his business. That's just the way it works. Anybody that goes out and fits into any category of person is the one that gets the lumps, whether you are a poor person or hard person. As my parents told me, "Always take the back seat, never take the front seat"—that way you don't have to be embarrassed by being pushed to the back. You will avoid being embarrassed.

The real man is *Macho—Macho* is when you are stubborn. It is a combination deal, somebody who is stubborn and yet with a lot of pride, "one-track mind" deal. Some parts of being a *Macho* are a good thing, for instance, if you want your home to work and you are determined to make it work. But if you are determined to "hold up the First National Bank," then that's wrong. If you are determined to get something being a *Macho*, regardless of how hard it is, you are going to work whether it's by force or by ideas. You can be *Macho* by using your head instead of your fists.

Paz has suggested that the Mexican always attempts to protect himself from the world. Manliness is associated with the idea of never cracking or backing down. Men who open up their hearts, who are submissive, are looked upon as traitors and are not to be trusted. The Mexican response to sympathy and tenderness is reserve, because the Mexican cannot tell whether such feelings are genuine. Furthermore, to respond to kindness is to be less masculine and threatens the individual's integrity. In the same way, confiding in another leads to a feeling of susceptibility or fear that one will be taken advantage of, and thus further demonstrate weakness.

According to Paz, the Mexican's quick anger is prompted by fear of being used by confidants, and also by the shame of having renounced solitude. He is defensive and always ready to repel any attack. The stoic or idealized male is able to comfortably keep his feelings to himself and thus is invulnerable. The *macho* is patient, impassive, and strong in the face of adversity, and while not overtly suspicious, he does not expose himself to the world. The cultural emphasis on form adds support to such a psychological position. As Paz has noted:

> The ritual complications of our courtesy, the persistence of classical Humanism, our fondness for closed poetic forms (the sonnet and the décima for example) our love for geometry in the decorative arts and for design and composition in painting, the poverty of our Romantic art compared with the excellence of our Baroque art . . . are further expressions of that tendency in our character. The Mexican not only does not open himself up to the outside world, he also refuses to emerge from himself, to "let himself go." (Paz, 1961, p. 32)

The ideal man is strong, virile, stubborn, a good drinker, good lover, good singer, good fighter, and brave and willing to defend that in which he believes. Shrewdness, keenness, efficiency, and success are also desirable. The ideal man has social grace, charm, and elegant manners. Intelligence and honesty are valued, as are kindness and charity, especially in those with positions of importance. Those with many women, who are independent and are willing to take chances, are also considered desirable.

Undesirable features include being a bully, abusing others, starting trouble, being dishonest, not paying bills or taking advantage of other people. Being dependent, parasitical, or agreeable for one's own gain are undesirable qualities. Individuals who do not assume their required social obligations are considered undesirable, as

77

are those who disgrace their family by being troublemakers, drunkards, or effeminate.

Homosexuality is severely condemned. Excessive authoritarianism is also undesirable, as are stinginess, selfishness, greediness, grouchiness, coldness, irritability, and excessive dependency. Lack of manliness, failure to understand one's tasks, and stupidity are also undesirable. According to Klapp, the *macho* theme

> makes Mexicans rather tolerant of the daredevil or plunger (arriesgado, arrajadizo, atrevido, aventado, intrepido) who sticks his neck out and does rash things. Although rashness is disapproved of, contempt for the opposite fault (miedoso) is so strong that a Mexican may prefer to be a reckless fool rather than a coward. (Klapp, 1964, p. 412)*

Like the ideal man, the ideal woman is secretive, prudent, and quiet. Here it is not fortitude but the view of women which reinforces the role they are expected to assume. Since women are the possessions of men whose task it is to transmit the values and energies of society, they are never asked about their feelings. Women are expected to ignore erotic stimuli, to be modest, tolerant, decent, stoic, and impassive. The *Mala mujera,* or bad woman, in contrast, is aggressive, impious, and independent.

It appears likely that many of the characteristics of the undesirable individual in Mexican-American culture and in Mexican culture do not vary much from undesirable characteristics in the Anglo culture. According to Klapp,

> though there are differences of emphasis most of these villain types do not tell much about cultural differences, indeed they stress the likelihood that the major categories of the villain are universal probably because the group functions (threatened by the villain) are universal. However, my impression is that Mexican vilification is more severe than American for certain categories

* Reprinted by permission from *American Journal of Sociology,* "Mexican Social Types" by O. Klapp, Vol. 69, pp. 404–414, 1964. The University of Chicago Press.

of behavior, such as male homosexuality and the emancipated promiscuity or fallen woman ; and that it is somewhat less severe towards rebels, revolutionist and Communists (izquierdistas—left-wingers—are not markedly vilified). (Klapp, 1964, p. 411)*

These considerations of some of the dominant value themes in this culture are of special interest for two important reasons, both of which dovetail with the practice of curanderismo. The values outlined above, while rendering support and direction to the general approach to life of Mexican-Americans, are in many ways mutually contradictory. That is to say, strict adherence to several of the themes we have considered lead inevitably to conflict, since such adherence requires individuals to strive for incompatible objectives. A case in point is the emphasis on group responsibility, obligation to one's family and elders, and adherence to certain patterned formalities—all of which are clearly at odds with the stress on individuality and independence that is exemplified in the *macho*. It is difficult to be a *macho* and group-oriented at the same time and individuals are frequently torn between loyalty to the group and independence. This struggle leads to exaggerated displays of manliness and courage in defying the norms of the group. A similar conflict arises between dependency on authority figures, which nourishes the strong dependency needs first generated in childhood, and the formal patterns of human relationships, which prevent adequate gratification of these needs. The latter, while protective of individual *dignidad*, as pointed out above, operate against fulfillment in personal relationships and at times intensify the need for further gratification of dependency strivings.

Such conflicts are reconciled to a great extent in the practice of curanderismo, which recognizes and legitimizes certain extremes of behavior as "sickness," thereby taking responsibility from the individual concerned. Excessive self-assertion to the point of antisocial behavior, extreme dependency, or helplessness, extreme withdrawal, and "helpful" involvement in the affairs of others

* *Ibid.*

79

beyond the bounds of propriety are all grist for the curandero. By virtue of being defined as "abnormal," they put the individual into the social role of patient, in which he is given opportunity to resolve the conflicts that have driven him to extremes and to return to the community with a more healthy perspective of the ambiguities of Mexican-American life.

As we shall see, the curanderos' therapies are sufficiently diverse as to permit the expression, albeit in different form, of many of these conflicts, thereby also encouraging reintegration. Thus, in that the curandero provides opportunity for the expression of intimacies (ordinarily barred from conventional relationships), dependency needs, and aggressive trends, he can satisfy a multitude of problems that cannot be satisfactorily dealt with otherwise.

VI

Psychological Conflicts of Mexican-Americans: The Severe Disorders

THE BASIC PERSONALITY PATTERNS and conflicts considered in the previous chapter are widespread among the Mexican-Americans studied and are encountered regularly by the curandero. It is the more serious disorders and folk illnesses, however, which constitute the vast majority of cases seen by the curandero. This chapter examines these in some detail.

In western medicine, diagnoses of both physical and psychiatric illnesses are made when possible on the basis of etiological knowledge. That is to say, a disease entity is said to exist when a specific agent such as a bacteria, a virus, or a toxin, produces a specific clinical illness. In many instances, especially in psychiatric disorders, such specific agents are unknown. In this case, disease entities are descriptively grouped on the basis of clinical observations of the characteristic symptoms, course, and prognosis.

The same general approach to diagnosis is followed by the curandero. The syndromes he works with correspond in many instances to syndromes recognized by modern medicine. Because his knowledge of physiology is minimal, he is likely to make mostly descriptive diagnoses, and usually they are solely on the basis of single symptoms. He is less inclined to group sets of symptoms into specific syndromes or illnesses. Some common diagnoses are: stomach-ache with nausea and vomiting attributed to eating "green apples" or to eating the wrong thing too fast; diarrhea from spoiled food; sunstroke from exposure to the sun which "causes a fire in head" and leads to "crazy talk"; tuberculosis (*tisico*); fever (*fiebre*); measles (*sarampion*); whooping cough (*tus ferina*); asthmas (*asma*); ulcer (*ulcera*); sore throat (*angina* or *mal de garganta*); cancer; appendicitis (*dolor de costade*); stones (*calcules*); worms in the stomach (*animalitos*), intestine, liver, and bladder; mumps (*mempes*); diphtheria; cold (*resfrio*); rheumatism (*rumes*).

In addition to these symptomatic illnesses, the curandero recognizes a number of illnesses manifested by symptoms not ordinarily grouped together in Western medicine. These are the focus of much anxiety, social action, belief, and ritual, and may justifiably be considered folk illnesses. *Empacho,* which can lead to abdominal swelling and death, is caused by undigested food in the intestines. The site of adherence to the bowel wall is marked by the site of breakage of an egg rolled on the patient's abdomen. Too rapid weaning may cause *caida de la mollera* in an infant, which is characterized by sunken fontanelles, fever, and apathy. This disease is believed to lead to loss of control of the brain and incontinence. This syndrome which clinically presents as dehydration can also occur if a baby is too roughly handled, or exposed to rain or cold air. *Susto pasada* is caused by fright and is manifested by bad digestion, gallstones, nausea, and vomiting. *Aire* is a term applied to earaches, stiff necks, colds, headaches, and dizziness and is attributed to air entering the body through one of its apertures. Severe cases are sometimes characterized by paralysis, twisted mouth, mental incapacity, or madness. These folk syndromes are empirically founded on commonsense observations.

To adequately investigate these folk illnesses, particularly those relating to psychiatric disturbances, it was necessary for one to decide on an approach to the data collection and data analysis which was comprehensive and feasible. There were several possible ways to examine data. I could determine to what extent the curandero recognized Western nosology or I could simply attempt to determine what categories of syndromes he used. Both such approaches have been used in previous studies of folk medicine. However, because of the desirability of maintaining uniformity of approach in this field, in order to facilitate cross-cultural comparisons, I decided to examine these concepts along the lines used by Devereux in his study of Mohave ethnopsychiatry and suicide. This is the most comprehensive study in the field of ethnopsychiatry to date, one which attempts to examine the data from a broad framework derived from a knowledge of both ethnology and psychodynamic theory.

The first category of disturbances examined was the disorders of the instincts. As we have seen, the control of emotion is a major concern of the child socialization experience, and is strongly reinforced by customs and values that emphasize formality and self-restraint. Difficulties in handling strong emotions, particularly antisocial impulses, are a major source of conflict in this culture, in part because of the great preoccupation with controlling these feelings, but also because the social system provides few acceptable channels for their release.

It was not surprising to find that disorders of the instincts were a major focus of concern for the curandero, who was firmly of the opinion that excessive feelings of hostility and of guilt over hostile feelings are significant causes of emotional illness. These feelings that were correctly attributed to difficulty in handling aggressive instincts and to the arousal of envy and jealousy toward specific people were thought to be important elements of emotional equilibrium. The curandero recognized and described people who had uncontrollable or pathological rages which had led to murder or violence. Their behavior was put down to jealousy and excess anger, which had overcome their minds. Similarly, repeated outbursts of rage or *choque nervios* were thought to be indicative of insanity or possession by the devil, and required incarceration or hospitalization to protect the community. While running amok and patterned ritual murders were not described among Mexican-Americans, epileptic murders and mass murders had occurred occasionally and were attributed to disease of the mind and stomach.

Nothing comparable to the cannibalistic windigo psychosis, which has been reported among the Cree and Ojibwa Indians, was described. That these did not occur was particularly interesting in view of the tradition of human sacrifice among the ancient Aztecs. (Hallowell, 1934; Landes, 1938) Myths and beliefs about ice- or stone-skinned giants, such as are found among Plains and Canadian Indians, also were not found. (Devereux, 1961) Similarly, no instances of lycanthropy were reported, although the curandero was convinced that the devil often masqueraded as a goat.

There is no scalping tradition among the Mexicans, as there is among the Indian tribes of the Southwestern United States. Lack of this tradition undoubtedly accounts for the lack of evidence for guilt over aggression directed against the outgroup and for the absence of special purification rites following aggression. Thus, aggression against oppressive Anglos was tolerated within the group and by the curandero. Ritualistic activity associated with fighting was not seen among those who fought in World War II, as it was among certain American Indian groups. Although no one believed that participation in the war had increased the risk of insanity, several curanderos expressed the opinion that exposure in Europe to venereal disease and immoral perverted sexual practices such as fellatio and cunnilinctus had been precursors of mental illness for Mexican-Americans overseas. While countermagic is used against witches, there is no tradition of witch hunts, as there is among some American Indian groups, and no instances of insanity following witch killing were described. Attempts at murder because of excessive feelings of jealousy or uncontrollable anger were, however, believed to lead to guilt and bad conscience and, in a number of instances, to mental illness.

Excessive activity is also believed to lead to emotional illness. Excessive studying and overwork, which are often crucial for social and material advancement in American society, are often criticized as being evidence of greed for money or status. Even strong individuals fear the censure and/or the envy of others in these areas. This belief is a particular problem for those eager to be acculturated to the American way of life and actively involved in an industrial community. Overactivity indicates that an individual is neglecting his Church and family for the sake of his own egotism. This is harmful in and of itself, since it increases one's risk of developing a mental disorder. Most of the activities that the curanderos considered undesirable when practiced excessively were in conflict with the Mexican emphasis on the status quo, the family, and the community, i.e., activities that could lead to acculturation. These activities are to be distinguished from another set of taboos, such as sexual perversions and incest, which too may lead to mental illness, or may by themselves be taken as indicative of mental abnormality.

Among curanderos, a more specific belief, which is also widespread throughout the world, is that individuals with special powers of healing or doing harm may become insane through misuse or excessive use of their power through self-seeking or ignorance. When this happens, it is thought to be an indication of punishment by God, rather than an indication that the power itself has taken control of the individual, as is sometimes believed elsewhere. Occasionally, insanity is believed to result from the individual's inability to tolerate the responsibility of such power. Individuals who are not divinely chosen but seek power for their own personal gain run the risk of insanity to the same extent as those who refuse power from God. By contrast, those who become sorcerers by obtaining special powers through pacts with the devil are believed rarely to be overwhelmed by their powers, since such powers do not reside within them but rather come from external sources.

When a curandero's ability to heal is corrupted through alcoholism, promiscuity, or immoral acts, he loses his power of healing, but insanity rarely follows (the opposite is true among the Mohave). This is important, since it is probably due to the fact that curanderismo is not a defense against serious emotional conflicts, as it is among certain groups. The absence of an emphasis on schizoid or trance-like states which, in other cultures, may attract emotionally unstable types to healing roles, is perhaps another factor reducing the use of this role for personal stabilization. In addition, curanderos rely mainly on empirical remedies and prayer in their treatment, and less upon special powers, which might require intense emotional involvement and might bring about an increased susceptibility to nervous disorder.

Supporting this conclusion was the fact that no evidence could be found for the belief that psychoses can result from the inhibition of magical powers. Thus while curanderos are undoubtedly motivated by various underlying needs to become healers, they need not undergo as much transformation of ego-dystonic conflict into role behavior as the healer in other groups.

Relating to Hippocratic notions of balance is the belief that the inhibition of emotions leads to their building up to pathological intensities. Transient agitated depressions or paranoid outbursts secondary to unexpressed jealousy are common disorders, which the curandero believed were due to such inhibition. The extent of the curandero's intuitive psychodynamic sophistication was demonstrated by his belief that depression, instead of paranoid violence, occurs when the individual fears the consequences of expressing his aggression directly or indirectly through sorcery. As we shall see in the discussion of treatment, the curandero wisely recognizes that the jealous individual must find a means for expressing his feeling in order to find relief.

Some of these psychodynamic themes emerged during the psychotherapy of a Mexican-American salesman whom I treated during the time I lived in Texas. It is instructive to examine this case in the light of the above considerations.

Antonio Gomez was born in San Antonio, Texas, to middle-class parents in February of 1921. He lived in this city until the age of six, when his family moved to Mexico. His early life was described as unhappy because, with five siblings, his parents were unable to give him as much attention as he desired. He began experiencing psychiatric symptoms as early as age five, when he was frightened one night by a barking dog. He lost his speech for fifteen days and remained fearful of the dark until late adolescence. Another significant early memory of the patient's concerned an experience at the age of eight, when, left in the care of an elderly aunt, he walked some five miles into a neighboring village without advising anyone of his whereabouts. When his father came to fetch him and discovered this, he beat the patient to the point of unconsciousness, accounting for, according to the patient, the fact that he has always stuttered and been fearful of people in authority. In addition to these symptoms, the patient has periodically suffered from fatigue, anxiety, and depression. The only favorable memory the patient had of the past concerned his early interest and talent in art. However, he never developed this, because his family was not in favor of it and a government scholarship was not forthcoming.

At the age of twenty, the patient returned to San Antonio to seek employment. He worked from 1944 to 1948 at various jobs. With the aid of a relative, he was able to obtain employment as a refrigerator salesman. In 1950 he joined the company with which he was still employed in 1964, and has worked steadily since then, save for a brief period in 1958, when he unsuccessfully attempted to establish himself in Mexico. Although the chicken farm which he opened was operating successfully, he felt obliged to leave Mexico to avoid his moral obligation to kill his brother-in-law who had presumably abused his daughter.

For various reasons the patient had little contact with his family through the years, save for his mother. Interestingly enough, he did as well as most of his family from a socioeconomic viewpoint. His oldest brother, George, was forty-six and worked as a contractor in Mexico. He was described as a quiet and serious person. The patient, forty, was next, followed by Gregorio, thirty-four, who also sold refrigerators in San Antonio. He was described as a quiet individual, concerned only with himself. Roberto, age thirty-two, who was as "emotional" as the patient, was the "only one who respects" the patient. He was an assistant manager in a large grocery. Julio, age thirty-one, was quiet and serious and also worked in a food market. Louisa, age twenty-six, was a San Antonio housewife whose husband was a newspaperman.

When first seen at the local mental hygiene clinic in January, 1961, the patient was anxious and insecure, occasionally stuttered, and expressed much concern over his inability to fulfill his expectations. He was particularly afraid that his feelings of anxiety and depression would affect his job to such an extent that he would not be able to care for his family. Testing revealed that he was of average intelligence. There was a noticeable constriction in the variety of his responses to stimuli, suggesting a narrow range of intellectual and cultural interests and a restriction in his use of imagination. He appeared to be more affected by the immediate aspects of his environment, to which he responded more on an affective level than on a more constructive, intellectual, evaluative basis. He also appeared to be too emotionally involved with his inner needs, which were being frustrated, and guided more by his emotions than his intellect. Testing revealed anxiety and some depression in connection with control of his emotional life, particularly in regard to hostile feelings, which took the form of increased concern with biological and anatomical matters, suggesting the potential utilization of phobic or psychosomatic mechanisms. The emphasis on feminine identification, as seen in the Rorschach Test, suggested the patient had had vacillating or at least ambivalent feelings in regard to a strong, dominating mother or mother figure, which he had generalized to all women. This also appeared to explain the clear, unresolved conflict in regard to his sexual role and the difficulty he experienced in his interpersonal relationships.

Severe distortions and contaminations in the thought processes and the emotions of the patient were lacking; it appeared that he was still able to adjust to the environment without distortion. The quality of his anatomical responses to the stimuli on the Rorschach Test and the high number of responses in regard to physiological and biological functioning on the MMPI also indicated the possible development of a very vague, unsystematized, paranoid notion, if he failed in his attempts to understand the causes of his feelings.

The underlying cause for his reaction seemed to be a feeling of being rejected and not having his dependency needs fully satisfied. There was also an unresolved conflict in regard to his own sexual role. The patient appeared to have a more feminine orientation combined with feelings of weakness and bodily concern. His generalized, vague feelings of impending assault suggested problems in sexual gratification. It appeared that he was handling his tension through repressive means and partially through hostile, open verbal expressions of hostility, rather than acting out.

The patient was followed for some nine months in the mental hygiene clinic by Dr. M., a Mexican psychiatrist, who used psychotherapeutic treatment and tranquilizers. During this period his symptoms of anxiety and depression fluctuated but never improved. After periods of improvement the patient often cancelled appointments. At the end of the year, the patient felt he had made no progress.

The content of his interviews varied from interview to interview but focused primarily on two themes: his domestic discord and his artistic, religious propensities. Discord had evidently become manifest shortly after marriage, when his wife's jealousy, high-strung nature, and materialistic orientation clashed strongly with his own unresolved needs for attention and affection. The interviewer noted that there was a tremendous hostility and ambivalence toward his wife, and that the patient was not as interested in sexual activities as she. Because of his indifference, his wife was inclined to think that he had other romantic interests away from home. When his wife visited the clinic, it became clear that she had developed a tremendous suppressed resentment toward her husband and that he in turn got depressed because of his feeling of being misunderstood or inadequate. The wife also felt that the patient took no interest in the upbringing of the family. She stated that he took no interest in the daughter's piano lessons and was indifferent to the progress the children were making socially and scholastically.

In addition to such domestic difficulties, the patient frequently made references to esoteric religious interests he had developed. He visualized the possibility of exercising his will power through a religious discipline which established him in direct relationship with God, but not necessarily within the dogmatic confines of the Catholic Church. He wished that his religious beliefs could extend to metaphysics and objective philosophy, that is, go beyond the limitations of Roman Catholic dogma.

The pattern of the patient's complaints continued over the succeeding year. The principle themes remained the same, although his conflicts over dependency and rejection were elucidated not only in relation to his wife, but also in relationship to his employers, his family, the Anglos, and the larger community. These conflicts proved to be a source of guilt because of the patient's inability to adhere to the culturally influenced ego ideal he had set up for himself.

The patient's basic problem appeared to be his excessive need for affection and approval from others, a need which made him dependent upon others and intensified his sense of inadequacy. This problem had roots in his early life when he received a minimum of attention from his busy mother, and his father, who although "generous and hardworking," spent much time chasing women. Shortly after his marriage, it became clear that his wife had excessive dependency needs of her own and was hard put to satisfy the patient's needs. In addition, she had been critical of his not working hard enough and not providing the family with luxuries. This dissatisfaction has served through the years to further alienate the patient from her.

Much as his wife was unappreciative, so too was his boss, for whom he had worked for fifteen years. The patient was on very familiar terms with his employer when he first started selling refrigerators. With the growth of the firm, relations between them became increasingly impersonal. The patient resented this for several years and felt that his boss has no "respect" for him, acted like a dictator, and didn't appreciate all that the patient had done. He felt the boss "knows my emotions and takes advantage of me."

In much the same way, the patient resented the fact that he and his family had been discriminated against because of their Mexican background, although he was tolerant of class discrimination in Mexico. This seemed to relate to the central theme of acceptance and rejection, which also affected his work. As the patient said: "I feel good when I sell refrigerators to people and they are pleased. Makes me feel good." This reaction contrasted strongly with his dissatisfaction whenever he encountered discrimination and felt "disgusted with the world—sometimes I prefer not to live in the world. . . . When somebody is happy with what I am talking about and interested in me I am happy. When I am happy and positive—people will open door. If I reflect sadness they will not. Something in my spirit they notice that. When depressed, they notice it."

In response to the frustration of his dependency needs the patient repeatedly experienced marked feelings of rage throughout his life, although he was never able to express these feelings satisfactorily. This impotent rage which appeared in depressive and somatic symptomatology also manifested itself in the patient's cynical views of nonaccepting people, whom he often described as hypocritical, discriminatory, and mean. "I didn't like lot of hypocrisy, vanity I see in people. I want to build perfect home." His underlying hostility was also manifested in his tendency to blame others for his failings, as when he was unsuccessful in early business ventures in Mexico, or when he left Mexico in 1958 after he discovered that his brother-in-law had made advances to his daughter.

In addition to the expressions of frustration caused by his unsympathetic wife, his selfish employer, and the discriminating gringos, the patient made frequent references to what he wished he could be. High on his list of valued qualities was the ability to control feelings, and he frequently alluded to his wish that his son would be a gentleman and his daughter a gentlewoman. This he believed was contingent on their learning to control their emotions and respect the ideas of others. Associated with adherence to this standard was what was described as a sense of pride and *pudor* (decorum) by which the patient distinguished himself from the *pilado,* or low-class Mexican.

Despite his willingness to ventilate his hostility and annoyance at the failure of his wife and employer to appreciate him, the patient had great difficulty in being directly critical of them and even more difficulty in examining his own contribution to the difficulties he described. It was similarly very difficult to get the patient to explore past attitudes and experiences with the purpose of enlarging the meaning of present experiences, for he seemed bent on describing his present gripes or the state of his mood.

The patient could not realize the importance of regular attendance. He frequently missed appointments, excusing himself on the grounds that he had some sales work in a neighboring county or that he was feeling "all right." Indeed, he had great difficulty in attuning himself to the notion of repeated and continual visits to get at his problems—and he saw treatment only as necessary when he wasn't feeling well. In addition, he made no effort to contact me when he was to be absent. Nor did he come on time for his appointments when he did come.

Of significance also during the treatment was the patient's reluctance to directly express any negative attitudes or feelings toward the therapist—a reluctance which appeared to be based largely upon the Mexican cultural patterns of obedience and respect for authority. This reluctance, coupled with the patient's inclination to be dependent, made it especially difficult to utilize experience in the therapeutic transaction for helping the patient to see persistent patterns in his behavior.

Throughout his treatment, the patient denied ever seeking the help of a curandero, although my own conversations with various curanderos suggested that his problem was a typical one and amenable to their methods.

A control of sexual instincts is as important as control of aggressive ones. In the sphere of sexual instincts, a careful distinction is made between sexual misbehavior, which is evaluated in moral and ethical terms, and disorders of the sexual impulse itself, which are seen in uncontrollable sexual urges and activity. The curanderos were unanimous in their opinion that sexual misbehavior was increasing and attributed this increase to the temptations of the city and to the work of the devil. By contrast, disorders of the sexual impulse are believed to be inherited from syphilitic parents or to be the result of anatomical factors such as a large clitoris. Such impulse disorders are called *furor* and are instances of insanity. Like the Mohave, the curanderos differentiate between an immoral promiscuous woman and a nymphomaniac who cannot control herself. The proper balance of sexual drives is believed to be very important for the maintenance of mental health. The damming up of sexual energies, as occurs in impotence or frigidity, may, it is thought, cause epilepsy or pseudo-epilepsy. Such a blockage may itself be caused by heredity ("passionate family"), bad food, excessive masturbation, and/or insufficient sexual activity. Excessive sexual activity, on the other hand, may drain the sexual energies and lead to priapism, weakness, and sometimes syphilis, as well as to perverse practices which in themselves are ultimately deleterious.

The curanderos are in agreement that women have more sexual freedom in San Antonio than they had in Mexico. The increased frequency of sexual experiences among them makes it more difficult for the curanderos to differentiate between sexual *furor* and sexual promiscuity. Traditionally, Mexican culture followed a "double standard." Men were tacitly allowed to demonstrate their masculinity through sexual exploits or by keeping a mistress. Women, on the other hand, were expected to tend to their homes and children and to tolerate their husband's behavior. Things have changed somewhat in San Antonio. The acquisition of greater sexual freedom by women has threatened the old patriarchal system. Men have responded to this threat by increased efforts to prove their virility through sexual activities. These simultaneous changes in the behavior of men and women have resulted in a general decrease in the stability of families. This decrease tends to weaken traditional role models for the young.

Relating to sexual activity is love magic, which is widely practiced and is often believed to be responsible for insanity in the victim, particularly as magic potions given to the victim to rouse his or her ardor may be excessive in their effects. It is among the first things the curandero considers when a young woman begins to act strangely. There are strong taboos against incest and it is believed to lead to insanity both in the victim and in the guilt-ridden attacker. *Nervios,* or nerves, is believed to be caused by sexual perversions such as fellatio and cunnilinctus, as well as by manifestations of disturbed sexuality such as premature ejaculations. Abnormal sexual habits are thought to lead to heightened sexual sensitivity. When such an individual is touched it is believed that the marrow of his bones comes out and produces a rapid orgasm. The "string" in the penis, or in the case of women, in the fallopian tubes, may burst from fellatio or other forms of abnormal sexual arousal and lead ultimately to loss of control of sexual energy. In women this bursting may lead to sterility or a "cold womb." Men may lose their ability to have sexual intercourse, may lose interest in life, and if sufficiently frustrated may "go crazy." While perversions lead to general conditions such as an imbalance of health, weakness, moral and emotional debility, "nerves," and sometimes insanity, the individuals themselves who practice such perversions are viewed as "mixed up" and as having defects of character, rather than specific forms of mental illness.

Another important group of disorders concerns problems of

mood. Much importance is attached to personal ties of friendship
and kinship in the maintenance of peace of mind, and mood disturbances following the death of loved ones are widely recognized
by the curandero. Symptoms of *melarchico,* which corresponds to a
reactive depression, include listlessness, sadness, anorexia, insomnia,
and tearfulness. Endogenous depressions and involutional melan-
cholias are not recognized as separate syndromes by the curanderos,
because a reasonable cause for depressive reactions can always be
found, and it is never necessary to hypothesize that they are due to
constitutional or hereditary factors. Depression following rejection
by a spouse is a variant of *melarchicho.* While it is considered a
natural and understandable reaction, it is explained by an elaborate
mechanistic concept which in effect states that "the nerves in the
head and the veins that go to the heart dry up and the heart
weakens and dries and then dies for a while." Depression is also
believed to follow from keeping one's worries to oneself, as was
demonstrated by one of the curandero's patients who silently
tolerated her husband's love affairs, allowing great sadness and
frustration to build up in her. Depression may also follow from a
guilty conscience, as in another patient who had an affair and continued to reminisce too much about it. Suicide was infrequent. This
was attributed to its being a sin, but a more likely explanation is
that the Mexican culture provides numerous direct and indirect
channels for the expression of aggression, so that unexpressed
hostility never builds up the same pathological intensity as it does
in more repressive cultures.

Love suicides also proved to be rare, probably because the
highly formal and traditional patterns of interaction protect people
from becoming too emotionally involved with each other. Thus,
sexual infidelity among women leads inevitably to violence among
men rather than suicide, while women tolerate infidelity by their
men.

The curanderos recognize delusions of worthlessness as
elements of depressions. As one said: "A man whose heart has
been broken is desperate, discontented, and suffers inside after the
death of a loved one." Depressions associated with paranoid

95

affective states are also recognized, and are seen in individuals who resent others looking at their wives. Such resentment may lead to unhappiness, a loss of interest in things, irritability, and the boiling up of feelings of anger and resentment which may ultimately explode in violence.

Depression is sometimes seen in association with shock or sudden fright. In this connection, one curandero described a woman who cried for four years after her son's death and always talked about him. People believed she could never be cured of this because the shock had killed her spirit and hardened her "nerves." Also some people who didn't like her continued to make her sick by always reminding her about her son. She cried all the time, lost weight, talked to herself, and frequently saw her son's ghost and heard his voice.

Depression is sometimes thought to result from the breakthrough in old age of earlier problems. The elderly are felt to have less adaptibility and less success in overcoming frustrations and the hardships of life than the young, who are strong and healthy with good minds and spirits. Depression in the elderly is attributed to constitutional factors such as aging blood, as well as to the persistence of bad habits such as masturbation. Symptoms of withdrawal, which are often seen in chronic schizophrenics sometimes have the appearance of depression. The curandero distinguishes this withdrawal from depression, viewing it as a form of insanity due to heredity, overactivity, or a weak constitution. Such chronic schizophrenic patterns are also distinguished from acute florid psychoses and are thought to have a poorer prognosis.

Of particular interest in view of psychoanalytic theories of dreams was the curandero's observation that insanity was often preceded by disturbing dreams. While dreams are not considered as etiological factors they are of some importance as prognostic signs. The cessation of dreaming occuring when an individual is "losing his mind" is a bad sign, since dreams are viewed as natural processes necessary for good health. Since the soul leaves the body and travels throughout the world gathering information during sleep, it is believed that dreams predict the future. Much attention is paid to particular dream themes. Significant dream themes are those dealing with the anticipation of the envy of others and appear to be a reflection of the dreamer's anxiety about community attitudes toward his behavior. Dreams of wrongdoing and punishment are common among individuals with troubled consciences.

In addition to these clinical conditions, the curandero recognizes a number of syndromes which closely correspond to Western nosological entities, although they may be attributed to supernatural factors, such as the devil, evil spirits, and witchcraft. While these conditions sometimes resemble those described above, they are considered to be quite distinct in their origins. Ghosts are one of the most frequent causes of acute transient psychotic states and anxiety states such as *susto*. They produce these reactions by possessing the victim and replacing his soul. The ghosts who are responsible for difficulties, or who are sent by sorcerers, are usually former enemies or deceased relatives and spouses who have not been honored on the Day of the Dead. One curandero described a patient who was unable to sleep because the ghost of his wife appeared before him every night. He recommended prayer and a special task for the patient to concentrate on which was designed to distract his attentions from thoughts of his dead wife. Devereux's explanation for the same phenomenon among the Mohave is of particular relevance for Mexican culture, where violence and aggression are not tolerated in the home and must be projected onto the alien world.

> The psychological transformation of the beloved relative's or spouse's ghost into a dangerous being is due partly to unconscious resentment over the beloved person's "desertion," and partly to the final eruption, triggered by the trauma of mourning, of the hitherto repressed aggressive component of man's unconscious ambivalence toward those whom he overtly loves. (Devereux, 1961, p. 134)

Witchcraft is another common cause of insanity and is usually invoked as an explanation for schizophrenic reactions and other psychotic disorders, including those with visual and auditory hallucinations and associated delusions. Such states are most likely to occur in individuals who are especially susceptible because of a bad conscience, physical weakness, or inadequate nourishment. The curandero recognizes paranoid reactions as due to the influence on the mind of the emotions, the spirit, and life experiences. Some people are believed to become abnormally sad and resentful from envying the more fortunate. Those who are envied may themselves become inhibited in their activities or suspicious of the envious and may develop paranoid reactions and ruminative and delirious states. Paranoid reactions sometimes also develop in those who blame others for their own inhibitions. This happens to shy men who explain their reluctance to pursue particular women as a result of something the women or others are doing to them. The curanderos also believe that the increased social freedom of women in Texas has accounted for an increase of jealous, paranoid behavior in the men. Suspicions of infidelity leading to verbal accusations or physical violence and then to fear of retaliation usually lead to even more intense suspicions. Fear of the jealous spouse and guilt over real or fantasied transgressions may also result in paranoid reactions in others involved in such situations. Grandiose delusions as compensations for poverty also are seen. A hebephrenic syndrome with silly, giggling, childish behavior and a cessation of mental activities is also recognized as a form of "nervous breakdown," which is intermixed with emotional and social deterioration during adolescence of previously normal children. As happens also in Western psychiatry, cases of mental retardation and behavior disorders are sometimes included in this category because of difficulty in differentiating them. Such individuals often break things, burn animals and houses, make holes in their bodies or in walls, poke their fingers in the eyes of animals, and do much harm to themselves and others in an abnormal way. This syndrome is thought to be due to a variety of causes including heredity, syphilitic parents, bad habits such as masturbation, the violations of cultural norms, and bad upbringing.

Hysteria in the form of excessive laughter, screaming, and

crying is often seen by the curandero, who recognizes this as a separate entity which he attributes to physical exhaustion or witch-craft. Frightening experiences also sometimes lead to attacks of hysterical anxiety associated with nausea, vomiting, and anorexia. Hysterical fugue states with withdrawal, bizarre behavior, and somnambulism occur and are thought to be due to excessive thought, worry, or overwork. No cases of hysterical anesthesia, globus hystericus, the latah syndrome of the Malay, the imu syndrome of the Ainu, echolalia, or echopraxia were known to have occurred. (Yap, 1951)

A fright in childhood is often thought to provide a major motive for unrealistic avoidances later in life. Such phobias are believed to be learned from parents rather than from the experience itself, since it is believed that children are only afraid of what they are taught to fear. There are a number of standardized and culturally acceptable objects of fear such as ghosts, witches and snakes. They provide individuals with ready-made, culturally acceptable fears, thus reducing the need to develop idiosyncratic fears and phobias. In addition, by expressing one's phobias in conventional ways, the individual increases his chances of getting help from others.

Obsessional states, which often occur in association with depression, were also recognized. Patients with these "always think the same things and never use their minds." Severe obsessional states are also associated with schizophrenia. The curandero was convinced that excessive preoccupation with a single idea could lead to an impairment of taste, smell, hearing, seeing, and feeling and ultimately to an incurable form of insanity. Obsessional states are of particular interest, insofar as they have been reported as rare in the less developed societies, which do not produce the type of character structure predisposed to such disorders.

Temporary trance states are rarely seen and are not highly prized or sought after, as in some cultures. While schizophrenia has been reported as rare in pre-industrial societies, numerous cases were reported and described by the curandero. The forms of this illness did not vary from those seen in Anglo patients, although there were numerous differences in the content of delusions expressed by schizophrenic patients. These reflected differences in Mexican beliefs and values.

An acute, transient, schizophrenic syndrome is often found. While it usually comes in relationship to specific experiences, it frequently follows excessive consumption of alcohol. It resembles the confusional episodes among African natives described by Carothers and the transient psychoses among the Mohave described by Devereux. (Carothers, 1953) The curanderos could think of only a few cases which progressed in time to chronic schizophrenia, as they did in acute episodes of *bouffee delirante aigue* in Haiti. (Sanseigne, 1961) These cases are sometimes initially confused with mania, which in fact is of much longer duration. While depression and mania are both recognized, they are not thought of as part of the same syndrome, even when they occur consecutively in the same person. As hypomanic mood swings are somewhat acceptable in Mexican-American culture, there is often no pressure to dampen one's exuberance, which in some situations sometimes intensifies the hypomanic reaction leading to mania. Many cases of hypomania, however, function adequately in settings that provide channels of emotional expression.

While the ability to "hold one's liquor" is a masculine virtue, there are strict restraints and social sanctions on excessive alcohol consumption and intoxication. This undoubtedly accounts for the low rate of alcoholism among unacculturated Mexican-Americans and higher rates among those who are actively seeking to reject their Mexican past and adopt American ways. The use of narcotics is also strictly taboo, but according to both the curanderos and public health authorities, is increasing in those urban areas where Mexican-Americans have encountered the most obstacles to acculturation.

Brief mention should also be made of a number of other conditions that were only rarely seen by the curandero. Psychopathic syndromes are usually reported as rare in preindustrial societies. The curandero did occasionally recognize some genuinely "bad people," who had either made pacts with the devil or had been born or brought up that way. Their behavior was not considered to be a manifestation of illness. Tics were not designated as psycho-neurotic disorders but were recognized as mild pathological phenomena, vaguely attributable to spirit possession. Mental deficiency was recognized as a disorder of the brain and was variously attributed to syphilis, heredity, infection, and physical trauma. It was difficult for the curandero to estimate the frequency of deficiency, largely because such patients, particularly if they were not disruptive to the life of the community, were rarely brought to him. That senile psychoses were rarely encountered may be attributable to the relatively short life expectancy of Mexican-Americans. In that Mexican-Americans have been inclined traditionally to accept and respect the elderly and give them a definite place in the social structure, it would be of interest to study in detail the effects of such attitudes on the development of senile disorders.

While a number of these familiar psychiatric syndromes are encountered and recognized by the curandero, the majority of psychiatric illnesses he deals with take the form of one of several folk illnesses, specifically, *susto, embrujada,* and *mal ojo.* These syndromes are of particular interest because the criteria for making diagnoses of them are flexible and are readily applied both to genuine psychiatric illnesses and to transient culture-determined and culture-specific reactions to conflict. This enables individuals with idiosyncratic conflicts to express their conflicts and symptoms in culturally standardized ways, which is significant in that it makes reintegration through the available cultural mechanisms possible for both very disturbed and mildly disturbed individuals.

People obtain group support when they can explain their emotional distress in terms that are culturally meaningful. The individual who is simply suffering from emotional symptoms does not get group support and is generally not thought to be in need of special help. This fact accounts for the large percentage of patients in the mental hygiene clinic and state hospital who have sought the aid of the curandero prior to entering. That is to say, the bulk of psychological symptoms are diagnosed in terms devised by the group and referring to the group's experience. Thus, many patients, even after hospitalization, continue to diagnose their difficulties using folk concepts, such as *embrujada, envidia,* and *susto,* which are acceptable diagnoses and referrable to the social and cultural context in which the symptoms arose.

Families are, in most instances, more concerned than the patient in making a diagnosis of a folk illness and seeking the help of a curandero. The underlying motivation for this is the desire to demonstrate that the illness is not due to faulty heredity, but to external factors not controllable by the patient or his family. That rejection of responsibility for the illness is of crucial importance is suggested further by the fact that the notion of punishment by God for moral transgressions is rarely invoked as an explanation for psychiatric illness. Further attesting to the role of the family in initiating culture-specific activities is the fact that most patients seen in the mental hospital had not sought the help of a curandero but had been taken to the curandero at the insistence of relatives. Another unexpected finding related to the fact that those patients who resorted to folk explanations were generally less sick than those who did not. This was particularly striking in the case of chronic schizophrenic patients, few of whom formulated their difficulties in terms of these culturally acceptable notions of etiology. Among schizophrenic patients, the extent of reliance on folk beliefs was positively related to their degree of psychological integration. When the deteriorative effects associated with the illness increased, the reliance of these ready-made explanations for disturbing subjective experiences decreased.

Fear of the evil eye is universal, and descriptions of it date back to antiquity. While it has been described in various forms by writers reporting on different cultures, among Mexican-Americans it invariably takes the form of *mal ojo,* an acute febrile illness accompanied by vomiting, listlessness, and excessive crying. It often strikes a child to whom affectionate overtures, without physical contact, have been made. Children wear bracelets, necklaces, or clusters of pink coral as protection against *mal ojo* and much effort is made to have all those who compliment a child make physical contact with him. If a meeting with a stranger had occurred previously, suspicion as to the presence of *mal ojo* is reinforced, as it is if the child dies. One curandero described *mal ojo* as follows:

> Fever and throwing up and real sleepy are the symptoms ; like they have tonsillitis or sore throat or something. Only they don't really have the tonsillitis. They don't want to eat. They throw up, especially milk or eggs. They have to get something cool in their stomach, something to slow it up. They create so much fever in their stomach that if they drink milk it will curdle. The evil eye is caused by somebody ordinary, like you or I, looking at the child and wanting to touch the child but not touching the child. The electricity of the person is sent off to the child. Some people have more than others. If the child is little it can't overcome this electricity until you cure it.

While all the curanderos adhered fairly closely to the same theory, some were willing to recognize the interchangeability of magical and medical explanations. These different views of the same phenomenon underline the importance of beliefs and values in determining which explanation is selected. As one woman said:

> Symptoms of *ojo* are kind of like a bad cold, except well on one side of your eye, awful headache, and they want to sleep all the time. They ain't got the strength to get up. If you think it's a virus, that's what it is, but if you create that it's *ojo,* that's what it is.

The psychological element involved in making a viral or febrile illness into a highly meaningful and culturally overdetermined pattern is suggested by the corresponding effects of *ojo* on others. It is generally accepted that the person responsible for the *ojo* will suffer a severe headache as long as the child is ill as a result of guilt. In addition, the mother of the child may also become sick at this time. As one woman said:

> If a child gets sick with these, the mother can have the same symptoms. They get chills and they may not feel well until he gets

better. It's like *susto* on the mother's part. When the child comes for treatment, the mother gets treated too if she's *asustado* and excited. The baby and the mother are doctored at the same time. Mothers usually get very nervous when their children are sick. Everytime a child gets one of these [*ojo, caida, empacho*] the mother usually gets upset too, particularly if she is the nervous type. The mother usually feels guilty that the child is sick. They fear that if they just would have been wise enough, they wouldn't a feed them no popcorn or anything, that causes *empacho*. Or if they get sick from *ojo,* she feels maybe she should stay away from the public. She feels better—at least, she doesn't feel guilty anyway.

Sometimes she gets so nervous, she tears up from it. My sister-in-law, everytime the baby gets sick, she gets sick all over herself, tears up, and so on. At night time, we went and got some popcorn, and I didn't even think about it with my baby. They didn't get sick, but she got sick and started to worry about the fact that they get *empacho,* so she had to go I don't know how many miles out of town to find the curandero she trusted. She thought it was *empacho*—the baby complained of pain for a couple of days. She claims she took him to the curandero and he got well. I imagine the more you think about it, the more created on your mind, the more it happens, more guilty you feel how your children are.

Mother-in-laws sometimes upset their daughter-in-laws by always saying "watch out, watch out," and fussing over them. I got a mother-in-law, but if my sisters were to nag at me about anything, I get upset. For instance, when I come to work and my kids get sick like happened four or five weeks ago, my sister nagged at me and told me, "If you stayed home and take care of them, this would not happen." So far as I am concerned, if they are gonna get sick, they are gonna get sick, whether I go to work or not.

Children will sleep with anything, whatever it is, whether it's *ojo* or just a cold. The mothers get excited over it. Of course there are different types of mothers. Some mothers can take a Tum and think everything will work out. Others get excited.

The more people think about it, the worse they create it. Not when they resent the children that these happen, it's when they love them too darn much . . . . When they love them too much and they are watching them all the time, never let them grow—you know, get on his own. A lot of mothers are like that; they

figure if he's gonna go outside he's gonna get sunstroke—if he
stays inside, you know, things like that. Women like this are
thought to be extra good according to their own book ; I don't
agree. Some people think these mothers are good, some of them
don't. The old people figure the kids were born to roll like a ball.
They have to get dirty, they have to get into trouble, and when
they get sick it's only natural—that's the way it goes.

There are two more complexes of folk ideas, behavioral patterns,
and practices focused predominantly on children. The first is a
clinical syndrome resembling dehydration, which is called *caida de
la mollera.* This syndrome also arouses much emotion in onlookers
and the community, for this, unlike *mal ojo,* is attributed to neglect
by the parent or person caring for the child. It was described as
follows:

> *Caida de la mollera* is when the hole in the front of a baby's
> head falls down, when you mishandle the baby and for some
> reason he can't suck, and can't hold his nipple. They lose weight
> because they can't eat and sometimes die.

More common than *caida de la mollera* is *empacho,* which
occurs primarily in children, but also at times in adults.

> It is caused by something to eat like popcorn or something
> else which babies don't digest and it sticks to the stomach. It
> sticks to some part of the stomach, I don't know which part. The
> next thing you know, they don't feel good and their bellies are
> running off. They get that from peanuts or anything that has hard
> skin, corn or peas, especially if they don't chew it good. It won't
> digest right, corn or chewing gum. Grownups get it too. They
> usually get sick when they eat onion and white cheese—*enchiladas*
> too. They get an awful bellyache and running off with diarrhea.
> Usually grownups can get it if they have had it before. They can
> get fever if it goes for a long time. Grownups don't die from it
> but small babies can. It don't happen when you are upset, it
> happens when you make the child eat something he don't like to.
> Sometimes it happens that way, sometimes it just happens for no
> reason. I don't know if the MD can treat it or cure it. I never
> know of anybody taking their kids to a doctor for that. They will

take a child for a cold but not for something like that. That they can treat with a home remedy. Doctors don't believe in *empacho*.

Mal ojo, empacho, and *caida de la mollera* are clearly associated with a variety of physical symptoms experienced by the child. These highly elaborated folk conceptions are of special interest because they not only define the medical problem and the necessary treatments and ritualistic steps that must be taken, but also serve to reduce the very great anxiety aroused by illness in a child.

In *caida,* we are dealing with guilt over neglect of the child, such as when a child is dropped or is thought to have fallen when not observed. In *empacho,* guilt is raised by the possibility of having given the child something "harmful" to eat. Whoever is blamed is not of primary importance. The significant thing is that something was done incorrectly. This feeling of guilt arouses many strong feeelings of hostility toward the child which, undoubtedly, exist in latent form in this culture where there is tremendous pressure on mothers to conform to the model of the perfect devoted parent. Both *empacho* and *caida* are associated with the proper management of children. Proper mothering is the focus of much anxiety, activity, and watchfulness on the part of others. This area is of special importance in this traditional culture where the weight of child training and education for adjustment centers almost exclusively on the home, and where great emphasis is placed on the conformity of the child to clearly defined age and sex roles. That the status of the parents, especially the mother, is very much tied up with the child, makes the parents somewhat dependent on their own children for the security and respect they obtain in this social system.

Ojo is similarly related to child care, but also includes a consideration of other individuals outside the family group. This relationship appears to be not only a projective maneuver but also a form of recognition of the fact that other individuals outside the family circle have upset the rather rigid and formalized arrangements of family activity. Thus, in *mal ojo* we find parental anxiety

Mal ojo explanation

and guilt being projected onto a stranger—perhaps one who has disrupted the customary routine of the household or has acted in a way to upset the normal balance of interpersonal relationships.

Because of his upbringing and the strong taboo on the expression of emotions, the Mexican grows up with much fear of his emotions, particularly hostile and sexual ones, and of the things that arouse these emotions. Emotion is often considered ego-alien or ego-dystonic. One solution for dealing with one's emotions is to retreat from the world of action to the world of words, which for the child has a magical and protective omnipotent quality. Thinking and talking are substituted for emotional expression and are skills important for Mexican-Americans to develop. Because thoughts retain much of the childish quality of omnipotence and because of the prohibition on action, the Mexican is inclined to accept the idea that thoughts can influence matter or reality and as such are dangerous. Thus, a concept such as *ojo* is in part a product of the belief in magic and in the power of words and rituals, a belief that corresponds in principle to concepts evolved during the primitive stage of childhood fantasy.

Related to *ojo* in the sense of acknowledging the introduction of outside influences are a number of folk complexes centering around the idea of bewitchment. *Embrujada*, brought about by *brujas*, or witches, is the most frequent of these and is usually the explanation given for incomprehensible behavior. According to one woman in the urban slum:

> *Brujas* are not usually old women. They are usually a young person. It doesn't make any difference whether you are good looking or if you have done well, there's a kind for every kind of emotion.
> *Brujas* don't have the power to cause the evil eye. They work altogether in a different way. They can do anything they want to start trouble. I have never seen a case. I wouldn't know what they look like if they are sick from the *brujas*. They claim that they pull their clothes off, or they pull their hair, or they hit whoever gets in their way. This is the same thing as *embrujada*—they claim

they got their groups, males and females, and they work together. One is a big *bruja* and all the others work under him. I find it mostly in Mexico that I know of. They say they work with a picture or something that belongs to the person, like a handkerchief or a piece of clothes. They claim there is difference; if you don't believe on it, he can't harm you. Or for instance you take my case—they once told me that some one was trying to fix me. But I never would believe in that now; I would never eat anything without brushing my plate first—that was back in 1947. Well, this lady, you know, I thought she was just trying to get some money. She told me that there was two men and one woman against me. She said, "You may get married, but I'm gonna tell you something —you ain't gonna be happy." I married in '49 and I never did put anything on it. I said that was bull-crap. I'll tell you one thing—I haven't been completely happy with my husband—sometimes what she said is on my mind. Maybe she wasn't so wrong after all; she never would tell me who the other persons were. I was sitting down there parked near the Santa Rosa Hospital, and I was just thinking about whether to go to the dance or not and she just come up. She was just a strange woman. Although I didn't believe her, sometimes it gets on my mind when things aren't going well. This woman I was with the other week, she went to a lady—I think she goes every week. This lady told her she was going to meet a guy who was going to show her a good time. After that she went back and she met some guy and it come true, I don't know how. Yes, she is married she didn't feel bad about it because the woman had told her this would happen. The victims of the *brujas* are usually people who are selfish, who want everything for themselves, who don't care about other people. People grow up to be selfish by not being taught to share and share alike.

Initial impressions suggest that individuals who are suspicious and moody, as well as those who begin to act in a strange way, are *embrujada*. In fact, this is not so. In most instances people who behave this way are felt to be "putting on an act," "feeling sorry for themselves," or merely trying to manipulate a situation for their own ends. The same behavior, however, if labeled *embrujada*, leads to a totally different set of responses on the part of others and a different manner of handling the individual. This is very much akin to our own dilemma in distinguishing malingering from genuine, unconsciously motivated, psychopathological behavior.

As one informant pointed out:

> If you are suspicious and angry, they just think you are imagining things, and that there is nothing wrong with you. You won't get treated. If some one is *embrujada,* they will get treatment from the family. The family will get together and make sure they get care. The family will plan and discuss it together. In my opinion, a person who is *embrujada* is really just suspicious, but they don't think so. If a person develops *embrujada,* even if nothing has happened, the family will look for something that happened because there must be an explanation, and they start running back over a few days or a few months. The ordinary doctor can't treat these things because the people don't believe that he can doctor them. They just figure the doctors don't understand anything about *embrujada* or *envidia* or anything like that.
>
> Some cases of *embrujada* get better ; some get worse. Some cases of *asustada* go on to become crazy. Every illness has it's length of time. In order to cure it, you've got to treat it in time. Some people, even if you treat them early go on and become crazy . . . if they are weak and they just decide they are not going to get well. Not everybody believes on this. Well, for instance when things go wrong with me, I think maybe it's a *castigo,* a punishment from God. I go to church and I pray to our God cause He's gonna show me the right way, for money, or sickness, or anything going wrong with the family. God has something to do with *embrujada* too. They feel that He has just left them out of His care.

In the course of this study, a number of hospitalized patients were interviewed. Special attention was directed to those patients who believed themselves to be suffering from the folk illnesses we have been describing. One patient who was *embrujada,* a twenty-year old mother of one, described frequent fights with her mother-in-law as the major cause of her difficulties. She was convinced that "somebody had put something" on her. She dated her illness to the time when she had returned to her parents' home to care for her sick father. Her husband at the same time had gone to live with his mother. He had become extremely jealous of the patient and frequently criticized her for talking with neighbors, for he thought gossiping might start trouble. During this time the patient became increasingly nervous and began to have hot flashes. She interpreted this as evidence that her mother-in-law was making her *embrujada* in order to get her to return to her husband. She described her mother-in-law as domineering and as eager to take care of the patient's baby. The patient had lived with her mother-in-law for several months after marriage, and was especially resentful of her mother-in-law's criticism during this time. The mother-in-law showed a preference for her own daughters and often was able to get the patient's husband to criticize the patient. The mother-in-law became angry when the patient expressed a desire to leave and the patient was fearful that she would be made sick if she didn't do what her mother-in-law wanted.

The psychodynamic features outlined in this case are of interest because of their almost universal appearance in this culture. One prominent element is the obvious dependency of the son upon his mother, even after marriage, which enabled her to interfere with the young bride and with the development of a feeling of mutuality between husband and wife. She did this by continually advising the bride on what to do and at the same time competing for her son's attentions. This relatively common situation is fraught with conflict and may be productive at times of severe emotional reactions. Furthermore, even when illness develops in such situations for other reasons, this ever-present conflict can readily serve as the focus for an explanation of the difficulty.

To understand how family problems can foster psychiatric difficulties, it is important to remember that the family is a most important institution for Mexicans. The persistence of the family organization is related to the continuation of authority and respect positions for different family members, e.g., the elderly who do not lose status as they advance in years, the idealized mother, and the feared father. There is much family pride and sense of affiliation with one's family. Individuals take great pride in the accomplishments of relatives even when they are not permitted to share in the glory. However, some family interaction patterns have limiting effects on family members, particularly if individuals object to the interference and involvement of others. Many young people are discouraged from establishing their own homes, ostensibly for economic reasons. This shared home thus permits parents and in-laws to continue to exert influence over them. Additionally, as is clear in the case above, many families are unwilling to accept their sons and daughters-in-law, considering them not good enough for their own children. While the potential conflicts inherent in such an institutionalized situation are somewhat minimized by the patterns of formality and respect, they are sometimes sources of resentment in and of themselves, especially where a daughter-in-law resents the fact that she is supposed to respect such patterns in relationship to in-laws. The hostility that is repressed and constrained by expected patterns is further complicated by the son's support of his mother, rather than his wife, because of his own deep-rooted sense of obliga-tion. It is also complicated by the birth of a grandchild, which gives the mother-in-law an opportunity to enter the situation as an "expert" who is kind and loving. The mother-in-law's apparent competence and warmth can set up impossible standards for the daughter-in-law. This can be particularly stressful for a young wife whose status depends largely on whether she bears children and how well she cares for them, considerations which often make her feel unnecessarily dependent on the child and perhaps resentful of him.

In this case of *embrujada* presenting in the form of a paranoid schizophrenic illness, it is not difficult to understand the sources of conflict. Living in a subtly hostile atmosphere which denied her expressions of autonomy and independence, the patient quite naturally developed hostile feelings, which conflicted with the well-demarcated role expectations for daughters-in-law. The culture requires strict adherence to a formalized code of conduct in a hier-archially organized, authoritarian family and social structure, and prevents the expression of hostile feelings directly. Angry feelings can be expressed only by displacement onto neutral objects or specially selected objects of projection—a fact which accounts for the necessity and widespread availability of projective beliefs.

Related to this is the fact that Mexican women derive their status from their husband's status and from strict adherence to customs associated with their roles. This patient's over-reaction to her role as daughter-in-law was interpreted by her not as a reasonable reaction to a tyrannical mother-in-law, but as a violation of group norms. As such, it was not only symptomatic of acute mental illness, but was a source of great guilt and anxiety to the patient and a reason for family reaction to the patient.

Since anyone can turn to witchcraft for such motives as vengeance, jealousy, hatred, and envy, Mexicans are forever fearful of being victimized, and are always careful not to arouse any of those emotions in others. This attitude introduces a certain conservatism among Mexicans and supports group values that stress acceptance of the status quo, humility, and nonaggression. Witchcraft practices thus are a means of expressing and controlling, in a certain social form, certain repressed desires, anxieties, and hostilities. Relief of tension by witchcraft activities also leads to improved social relations, by reducing these repressed emotions.

The Mexicans are noted for their sharing, their cooperativeness, and their lack of aggression toward one another. The suppression of aggression within the group is especially desirable in maintaining the stability of the group. Even the person who causes evil eye is considered to be unaware of what he can do and is therefore blameless. The belief in *embrujada* explains disease and misfortune on a conscious level, and magical practices provide techniques for dealing with anxiety underlying this belief by permitting the expression of socially harmless aggression. At the same time, common beliefs and shared practices bring the group to a greater solidarity.

Since the amount of anxiety expressed by witchcraft is a function of both the intensity of social conflict and the degree of expression, one would expect a decline in witchcraft with an increase in the number of social channels for behavioral expression of aggression.

This is indeed what one does find among Mexican-Americans in Texas, although the belief in witchcraft continues to persist.

It is interesting to note that accusations of witchcraft do not occur randomly in the social system but occur in association with what may be considered areas of stress. *Patrons,* other wealthy or respected individuals, and Anglos are rarely considered responsible for witchcraft, perhaps because few strong feelings are engendered toward people who are socially removed from the victims. At the same time, accusations against family members are rarely made—suggesting the extent of repression of hostility within the family. Accusations against the family are frequently made, however, by acculturating individuals who may attribute their bad luck to bewitchment by their relatives. Prospective spouses or in-laws are also frequently accused of witchcraft since accusations of witchcraft legitimize an individual's withdrawal from an engagement without losing face.

One often hears witchcraft accusations made by young wives against mothers-in-law, who may actually be trying to influence their grandchildren's upbringing or may be preventing the son from being freely involved with his wife. Young wives may be subject to considerable strain in relation to their mothers-in-law and other members of their husband's families.

While *embrujada* may be caused by anyone, man or woman, the witches are more commonly thought to be women, much like their European counterparts, who can fly at night and take on the form of animals. The witch is the opposite number of the good woman, onto whom are projected a number of passive-dependent and ego-alien feelings and needs, which are incompatible with *machismo.* The witch tries to dominate, seduce, and weaken man. Her efforts to control his mind and behavior may reduce him to a childish helplessness, which is a longed-for but prohibited state. Since dependency needs cannot be condoned in this culture, men can be passive and dependent only when they are bewitched or sick.

Individuals are thought to be bewitched when they demonstrate socially undesirable characteristics such as outspokenly sexual, aggressive, or jealous behavior, when they have lost control of their emotions or impulses, or when they are mentally disturbed. A closer examination of the bewitched suggests that they are rarely innocent victims, but rather that they have usually violated some norm or social expectation by excessive aggression, success, or improper respect, and thereby have provoked the witch or the envious to act against them.

In some situations, the development of abnormal symptoms can be related to particular social and interpersonal events. Thus, violations of status restrictions, traditions, or any of the complex, formal, interpersonal patterns of respect—knowing one's place, humility, and the acceptance of God's world—either arouse anxiety and initiate a vicious circle of guilt and anxiety, or are focused on retrospectively as possible explanations for severe emotional disturbances. These comprehensible situations involve the concept of *envidia* instead of *embrujada.*

There is some suggestion that illnesses are more likely to be explained by *embrujada,* while misfortune and bad luck are more likely to be explained by *envidia.* However, closer examination reveals that the social situations in which the two occur are different, although the mechanisms are essentially the same. As one man said:

Envidia—that means somebody envies you and they try to ruin you. . . . Whether you have got a good house, or a good marriage, or a good garden. People are afraid of *envidia,* when they start going downhill, like when they start losing their house, or marriage troubles, then they think some one must have envied them. It doesn't mean they get sick, it just means you've got bad luck. *Envidia* mostly appears to people in the same neighbourhood or the same town. Like you take a couple of kids that grow up together—one does better than the other one. If this person doesn't like what the other one does, they go to a *bruja* or curandero and fix it where he will lose everything, whether it's his business or his diploma or something. They lose it because this woman puts a spell on them, using a picture of them or a handkerchief. *Envidia* is the same thing as *embrujada* except the person isn't sick. He is just having bad luck.

Envidia is really in the person's own mind. When a person tries to take too much, he feels guilty—sometimes it does happen that someone has actually put the spell on them. I got a feeling that *embrujada* is the same thing when a person feels guilty—it's like giving somebody else the rap for what you did yourself. They won't admit it though. Most times when someone's got *embrujada* and you look closely, you find something they have done wrong, and they don't want to admit to it. Now my sister-in-law she went to a mental hospital and they gave her up for good, but she still believed that it was *embrujada* and that her husband got her that way. Well, he beat her up a couple of times, she figures she wasn't going to take it anymore. She also ran around with some other man ; she never did like her husband. She was living with her mother-in-law. She fought with her mother-in-law. Her husband stuck up for his mother. She had a nervous breakdown but she wouldn't admit it. They took her to a curandero and the curandero couldn't get her well, and for some reason, they just put her in a mental hospital. They gave her an electric shock and that got her back on her feet.

To reduce interpersonal tensions, one consciously develops superficial charm, and the skill of appearing self-sufficient and complacent. These help individuals to avoid being taken advantage of by others. These skills also lead to an avoidance of criticism and enable individuals to tolerate the authority of others by reducing the sense of personal subordination. The reverse side of this is the apparent unwillingness on the part of Mexican-Americans to give orders and accept responsibility—a trait which derives in part from the overemphasis placed in this culture on adherence to role and form as opposed to initiative and self assertion.

Fear of the envy of others is an exaggeration, which derives in part from the large, extended family relationships where individuals learn not to exceed the limits of their roles. When individuals begin to succeed, they often feel guilty, arousing latent anxieties about being punished for outdoing siblings and parents. Guilt over violating group expectations may then be projected onto those people who are both hated for preventing the individual from doing what

115

he wants and feared because of punishment expected from them. Through such projection of his own reluctance to act in contravention of the status quo, the individual blames others and thus becomes the object of his neighbors' or relatives' envy. This situation may lead to progressive anxiety or may simply be used as an explanation of an already ongoing psychological reaction.

A not uncommon theme among hospital patients was a fear of neighbors and a tendency to blame difficulties on them. Many patients were convinced that the envy and witchcraft of neighbors had produced their symptoms. This recurrent theme points to a major source of friction, the interference of neighbors, parents, and relatives. This observance is reinforced by numerous beliefs ascribing severe personal disorganization to the overwhelming influence of the unusual powers of others.

It is partly because of the exaggerated view of the potential harmfulness of others that individuals are constrained in their personal relationships and are especially formal with strangers, as has been noted previously. Some have close friends only within their extended family. Such an ideal pattern is difficult to maintain, however, because of the marked overcrowding in the Mexican communities and also because of the real inclination of people to be dependent upon the help of neighbors. The generosity, joviality, and friendliness of Mexicans thus exists in the presence of vague, unclear fears that one will be taken advantage of by others.

It is of interest in this connection to mention a few of the other delusional themes frequently encountered among hospitalized Mexican-Americans, which, too, were rooted in the predominating beliefs of this culture. Food, which is a major source of feeling and interpersonal relations among Mexicans and an integral part of the hot-cold concept, figures prominently in many delusions about being poisoned. Many Mexican-Americans are reluctant to eat in unfamiliar places for fear of possible physical harm from eating "new and strange" foods. Religious ideas also figure prominently both in explanations of illness and in delusions. One woman heard God's voice talking to her and became convinced she was the

Virgin Mary, a common theme among Mexican-American women with psychotic illnesses. Her life had been hard and she felt she had sinned against God. She became increasingly depressed, anxious, and self-accusatory and could not function adequately in her role as wife and mother until she heard the voice of God speaking to her. From this experience, she became convinced that she was the Virgin Mary, a delusional idea the acceptance of which served to reduce her anxiety and distress by providing her with an explanation (albeit false) of her experience.

These ideas, which also figure prominently in the complaints of neurotics, relate to certain regular patterns of authority and traditionalism in this culture. Exaggerated feelings of being controlled by significant persons lead naturally to ideas of influence, usually through such culture-specific vehicles of control as witchcraft, magic, and poisoned food.

Sexual themes are expressed in terms of unfaithfulness, jealousy, fear of homosexuality, and impotence in men; hyper-sexuality and virginity in women. These themes clearly relate to the rigid sex-role differentiations found in this culture and to the severe repression of self-assertiveness and sexual and emotional expression in men and women.

Delusions of ghosts clearly seem to be tied up with conflicts over hostile feelings toward parents who have died; these feelings conflict with the expected attitudes toward parents. Similarly, feelings of being controlled by ghosts or female witches were found to relate to and to derive from underlying resentments of domineering, controlling mothers or mother surrogates. Fears of *brujas, embrujada,* and the devil appeared to be related to resentment over paternal authority; this resentment was projected and displaced onto culturally acceptable symbols. Expressions of jealousy were found to relate to unsatisfied love for the father; resentment of siblings was often expressed in the terms of neighbors being envious; and unresolved Oedipal and sexual identification problems were expressed in terms of jealousy attacks or possession by the devil.

Thus, delusions relate to affects such as hate of mother, love of father, and hate of siblings, feelings which cannot be expressed in conventional ways but must be projected onto culturally available symbols. More direct expressions of hostility are also permissible when the individuals are wittingly or unwittingly associated with some form of magical activity.

The study of beliefs and delusions is of value in pointing to sources of strain in the community. Such a study is especially valuable because both commonly held beliefs and delusions derive from the same sources and serve similar purposes, both for normal individuals and for the emotionally disturbed. The difference is one of degree only. It is also possible that one may distinguish the degree of severity of a schizophrenic illness by the extent to which individuals develop idiosyncratic delusions as opposed to culturally specific delusions. This is clearly seen when one compares individuals suffering from acute schizophrenic illnesses to those with more chronic, progressive forms. The latter often manifest delusions that bear little resemblance to the beliefs of the group.

One of the most common forms of folk illness throughout Latin America is *susto* or spirit loss. As would be expected, it is frequent among Mexican-Americans and accounts for a good deal of the curandero's work. Unlike *ojo,* *embrujada,* and *envidia,* it occurs less often as a result of direct interpersonal experiences and more often merely as a result of personal experiences with which individuals are unable to cope. The symptoms of *susto* are a mixture of anxiety—dyspnea, indigestion, palpitations, and depression—loss of interest in things, irritability, insomnia, and anorexia. According to one curandero, it often leads to heart trouble (heart attack), peptic ulcers, and mental retardation. It occurs most often following the death of a loved one or a frightening experience. According to the curandero:

> Fellow have a wreck. This woman saw this man die and then lost her voice and then she saw ghosts. You have to use your mind. She choked for five to ten days with shaking and then the ghost

went inside her. She had a shock. After she tells what happened she is better. Must ask for the truth. Ghost goes into mind and right sense leaves the body.

Another informant said:

They claim the spirit or the soul leaves the body. I guess they just get shook up and that makes the soul leave the body. Just plain scared, you know, shook up. People who are more nervous are not more likely to become *asustado*. *Asustado* is one thing, being jumpy is another. When a person becomes nervous they do a lot of hollering and if they are after the kids, they are going to knock the daylights out of the kids. If you are *asustado* that means someone scared the daylights out of you, like trying to run over you with a car. When my brother dies, my sister-in-law became *asustado*. She must have had it for fifteen days. She was just jumpy. You could walk in the door and she would just jump. I don't know—I guess she was figuring on seeing my brother walk in. The soul isn't left around after the person dies. I think that's mostly your conscience. No dead person is gonna come back. People often start hearing things and seeing things as if the person was still alive. Some people think that the dead come back and interfere with their lives. They think about that a lot and they get sick. Sick to where they either lose their mind or they just be a nervous wreck. The best thing to do is to throw that person over sight [i.e., forget them]. People create that the person who died is around, and they will get sick from that. The next thing you know, they have to get treatments, or they lose their mind. People accept those who are nervous. When someone is nervous, the people take it for granted, and they say "Oh, she is just putting on an act." Most people think the person who is nervous is putting on an act because they want attention. They won't give them the attention that they want, and we give them attention when they have *asustado* and try to doctor it. Persons are better off having *asustado* than just being plain nervous. Both look the same.

These points were illustrated by the case of a twenty-four-year-old factory worker who was brought to the hospital by his mother with symptoms of tension, anxiety, and depression. These had been brought about by fears that he was no longer a man and that others who thought he was "queer" were threatening to homosexually assault him. He believed he was *asustado*. He had been involved in a number of passive homosexual experiences as a boy and a number of aggressive homosexual acts when intoxicated during adolescence. He lived in his mother's house with his wife, an aggressive woman, who criticized him for being shy and self-conscious. Throughout his life he had felt that his alcoholic father had mistreated his mother, to whom he was especially attached. This case was reviewed with the curandero who said:

> I would call that *susto*-excitement, because he was overprotected by his mother. It makes him feel guilty, you know, ashamed —he wasn't grown up. There was nothing wrong with him. He wasn't on his own. That makes him feel less a man than the next man. It is important that the mother lets him on his own and learns to trust him. Also, that the wife let the man be on his own, otherwise the man is shocked.
>
> When a child gets to be a teenager, he wants to be trusted. It works in both boys and girls, and when they make a decision, even when they get older, they think they have to get hold of the parents, or the kinfolks. Spirit never develops to be strong. In other words they ain't got the guts to stand up . . . . His father had something to do with his condition. He grew up in fear of his father. He resented his mother to a certain point because she wouldn't fight back. He was afraid to fight because he was supposed to respect his mother.

The conflicts of this patient are similar to those of many men in this culture which fosters infantilization of the children by the mothers and rejection by the fathers. By being encouraged to sympathize with his mistreated mother and to reject his father, this patient had little chance for making a strong, masculine identification. Because of his sense of responsibility and respect for his mother, he was not able to express independence without feeling that he was rejecting his mother. His inability to be assertive in relationship to his mother was intensified in relation to his domineering wife, and raised the fear of homosexuality in his mind. Projection of this fear led to the delusion of being assaulted and a condition of tension, depression, and anxiety, which was explained in terms of *susto* or soul loss.

Virility is important for the Mexican male and is expressed in *machismo* or in the Don Juan pattern of repeated sexual conquests. These patterns are permitted and condoned even among married men, except when they are accompanied by brutal, improvident, irresponsible, or inconsiderate behavior. A strict differentiation of sex roles supports these attitudes. Men serve strictly instrumental needs; women, expressive needs. Such strict role differentiation leads to numerous conflicts associated with the adequacy of role performance, because of the obvious difficulty in behaving in conformity with a model of human behavior which is so polarized. Thus, one finds much anxiety about being a man, which is expressed in terms of homosexual fears, as in this patient, or in terms of excessive sexual exploits. This anxiety compares to the marked anxiety about the maternal role found in the case of *embrujada* discussed above.

Such role differentiations are more clearly seen when viewed in contrast to the Virgin Islands, where a comparative lack of differentiation of social role by sex is correlated with a relatively low incidence of sexual themes in psychoses. As with the French, Continentals, and Puerto Ricans in Weinstein's recent study, sexual delusions are more common among Mexican males than females and usually are associated with themes of jealousy. The male's preoccupation is more with what women will do, and less with his own sexual failure and impotence.

Sexual themes were not uncommon in the delusions of Mexican patients. These themes are expected in a culture where there is a classification of the environment in sexual terms and a marked differentiation of social roles according to sex. In such cultures, identity is gained in terms of "masculinity" and "femininity." Sex is equated with sin and virtue. As Weinstein has suggested, in "sex-oriented" societies, such as Mexican society clearly is, the probable high incidence of sexual delusions does not mean that they are the manifestations of the loss of control of biological drives or instincts, or a regression to infantile styles of sexual expression. More important are the stereotyped concepts of masculinity and femininity and the patterning of the roles of father and mother.

Susto, which commonly occurs among individuals about to be married, appears to relate to sexual anxieties and Oedipal conflicts. The desire to be a man and the fear of being overwhelmed and castrated are significant here, as are the arousal of aggressive impulses. The individual's fear of his own impulses is also related to the self-destructive attitude toward women, which may be turned against the self, thereby arousing a fear of death in some individuals.

The fear of illness or death, which is commonly associated with *susto,* is clearly related to these psychodynamic features. Psychoanalytic studies have shown that certain childhood experiences may turn a fear of castration or loneliness into a fear of death. Thus the idea of death associated with *susto* may contain elements of anxiety about punishment for death wishes against others, as well as anxiety about one's own excitement. This is reasonable in a culture where impulses must be controlled at all costs and where hostility to authority is strongly dampened by the strict patriarchal hierarchy.

The diagnosis of *susto* and other folk illnesses is not always clear-cut. A number of patients were variously thought to be suffering from *susto, embrujada,* and *envidia,* suggesting that these concepts were interchangeable in describing a single psychological event or illness. More important, however, is the fact that a number of different folk illnesses may result from the same situational conflict or interpersonal stress, depending upon the roles of participants as well as upon their basic personalities. The curandero makes a diagnosis on the basis of the presenting symptoms and clinical picture and on the basis of the history, not on the basis of symptoms alone. Diagnosis is not a static category for him, but a dynamic formulation of all the relevant information and observations. Thus, a diagnosis of *susto* may be made in the presence of depressive, neurotic, or even schizophrenic symptoms. The diagnosis is really based on whether a history has been obtained that the individual has been frightened by some experience early in childhood or later on, in adulthood. Similarly, a diagnosis of *embrujada* may be made in the presence of symptoms of schizophrenia, extreme suspiciousness, or even anxiety. This diagnosis rests in large measure on the history of someone having tried to do harm to the patient. The same symptoms may lead to a diagnosis of *envidia,* if they occur when others envy the patient but have made no active effort to cause harm, i.e., they may have only wished him harm. Thus the identical clinical picture may lead to the different diagnoses of *asustado, embrujada,* and *envidia.*

VII

Diagnosis and Treatment

WHILE THE COMMON MALADIES are handled pragmatically without too much social action or theorizing, noncurable and strange illnesses provoke much anxiety. They bring to the surface normally latent anxieties and fears, intertwined with explanations about the illness. The family and the curandero will try to determine whether a sick individual has violated the commands of God, incurred the wrath of an enemy, or simply come into contact with a witch or an evil person. In evaluating the history of the patient's illness, the curandero considers his behavior in relationship to his family, his habits, and his temperament. When this information reveals no obvious reasons for the patient's difficulties, more supernatural explanations are invoked. The social group plays an active role in making the diagnosis. The family may present an etiological hypothesis on which the curandero will elaborate in line with his knowledge of the patient and the presenting syndrome. The entire process is quite complicated.

The sick role is an acceptable role but, as Parsons has shown, a deviant one. People are initially reluctant to be classed as sick for fear that illness may lead to a loss of respect; this attitude accounts for the value placed on *machismo* and female stoicism. (Parsons, 1951) Denial of illness is common and often patients are very ill before they seek help. Conversely, sickness is taken very seriously and the sick are excused from their usual responsibilities and from their obligations to adhere strictly to norms. Illness is a reason for inaction and justifies both passivity and dependency without loss of esteem, with an increment of love, respect, consideration, and indulgence.

To overcome the difficulty in accepting the sick role, the group actively participates in treatment, which helps to minimize the patient's sense of losing respect. It is important to note that individuals do not feel guilty about becoming sick in the sense of feeling responsible for their illness, but rather are ashamed to admit their inability to suffer pain and distress. The supportive treatment individuals receive, and the reduction of responsibilities, are important secondary benefits of the sick role, which may unconsciously contribute to the development or perpetuation of illness in certain individuals. The entire family participates in decisions about medical action, contributes to the medical fee, and assumes certain of the patient's duties and responsibilities when he is ill.

Although the role of the family found here clearly differs from that found in modern medical practice, many of the curandero's procedures are actually very similar to those of the Western physician. The curandero first takes a history of the present illness, either from the patient or family, systematically asking about various possible symptoms in different systems of the body. If necessary, he inquires as well into the social and domestic life and occupational experiences of the patient. Particular attention is focused on appetite, sleep patterns, fatigue, and energy level, and the presence and location of pain. In estimating his general state of health, he next examines the patient's facial expressions, bodily movements, and coloring. He then palpates the patient's body for tenderness, soreness, inflammation, or tumor masses. He takes note of fever, paleness, flushing, anemia, jaundice, and the strength and speed of the pulse.

Because of his lack of knowledge of modern pathophysiology and etiology, he often cannot accurately assess the syndrome at hand. This is especially so in the case of diseases requiring moderate laboratory methods of diagnosis such as endocrine, neoplastic, and hematopoietic conditions, although these admittedly constitute but a small proportion of syndromes presenting to the average Western doctor.

The establishment of a diagnosis in modern medicine is a highly complex act, relying on anatomical and pathophysiological knowledge, as well as on clinical experience. While the curandero's pathophysiology is based on Hippocratic humoral theory and his knowledge of anatomy is rudimentary, he is often correctly guided by his clinical experience in determining a diagnosis and is sophisticated enough to correlate symptoms and signs with a disturbance of underlying function. Because his conceptual scheme of disease differs from that of Western medicine, the various combinations of signs and symptoms are constituted into different syndromes. Since many diagnoses are symptom diagnoses, these differences are rarely apparent. Thus, stomach pain may be diagnosed as stomach pain with no further attempt to delineate a specific etiological agent. Similarly, diagnoses such as coughing, vomiting, swelling, pain in the head, and diarrhea are often made. Such an orientation makes it especially hard for the curandero to accept a diagnosis in the absence of symptoms. This orientation accounts, for example, for the unwillingness among Mexican-Americans to think a person has tuberculosis in the absence of symptoms.

In the absence of modern medical knowledge and modern laboratory equipment, diseases of internal organs are more difficult to delineate than are, for example, psychological disorders which are readily observable and which lend themselves to descriptive detail. Similarly, wounds and external injuries are well recognized and described. In some instances, as in the case of tuberculosis, the curandero can be of some help in giving sound advice, recognizing as he does the importance of mental state, living conditions, and diet, even when he is ignorant of the tubercle bacillus. With psychiatric and psychosomatic illnesses he is on a much better footing, for he is cognizant of the influence of such factors as dammed-up libido, excessive guilt from taboo violation, group rejection, jealousy, envy, hostility, and fear, in the production of illness. He is also aware of the beneficial effects of love, hope, and faith.

It is of interest to examine the approach to psychiatric diagnosis in more detail. While psychiatric diagnoses are based on descriptive criteria, this is not altogether bad, particularly in regard to a functional psychosis like schizophrenia. As recently as 1911, Bleuler defined schizophrenia in descriptive terms of specific symptoms of feeling, thinking, and behaving in relation to the external world. (Bleuler, 1950) Others, such as Kleist and Leonhard, maintained that diagnosis in cases of schizophrenia must be postponed until a defect state is observed many years after the original attack; still others, such as Menninger, have argued against the value of diagnosis (Fish, 1962; Menninger, 1963) The fact that the curandero makes an intuitive diagnosis on the basis of his experience should not really be cause for criticism, particularly if one thinks in terms of Jaspers' concept of "understandability." (Jaspers, 1964) Here the physician determines whether a symptom is understandable by empathizing with the patient and assessing whether the symptom logically or emotionally could arise from the patient's affective state, previous personality, or current life situation. Using such an approach, only incomprehensible symptoms are considered schizophrenic. Curanderos are often criticized by those who expect that the determination of the etiology of psychiatric illness should follow the model developed in the study of infectious diseases. Because certain microorganisms have been shown to be responsible for specific illnesses, specific etiological factors in the causation of emotional disorders have been thought to be the only acceptable explanation. While this approach has heuristic merits, it neverthe-less leads to a minimization of other considerations such as socio-cultural, genetic, and climatic factors, which also may play a part in host susceptibility and resistance, and which are crucial to the curandero's frame of reference for physical as well as psychiatric conditions.

The curandero's view is akin to Meyerian psychobiology, which held that schizophrenia developed in a person with a special per-sonality and constitutional susceptibility, who had developed a habit disorganization secondary to lack of adaptation to the cus-toms and cultures of his group. (Meyer, 1951) For the curandero, as for Meyer, schizophrenia does not develop *de novo,* but is related to, and understandable in terms of, the individual's personality and life experiences. The good healer recognizes the significance of hereditary factors in the development of emotional illness and is aware of the importance of social contacts, active participation in life, and expression of emotion, as well as the deleterious conse-quences of broken homes, divorced parents, maternal deprivation, social isolation, and psychological stress.

Thus, the curandero works within a system of certain rules, although he relies upon supernatural as well as natural ideas to explain questions of how and why people get sick. His approach is similar to that of psychiatry, in that, as Fish has noted:

> psychological events can arise out of other psychological events in a way which we can "understand." . . . In the individual case, the decision about the reality of a given understandable connection depends on whether or not it helps to form a coherent picture of all the objective material available to the observer, such as what the patient says, his modes of expression, his spiritual works, his style of life, his actions, and so on. (Fish, 1962, p. 130)

This understanding psychology leads naturally to interpretative psychology, in which knowledge gained by understanding is sys-tematized with the help of concepts borrowed from philosophy, psychology, neurology, or folklore. The explanations, used both by the psychiatrist and the curandero, are actually hypothetical concepts that enable them to predict events to some extent, but hardly with the accuracy of engineers or natural scientists.

Often psychiatrists confuse scientific or actual causal relationships with understandable ones derived from their interpretative psychology. It is clear that the curandero functions on the same level, although he has recourse to a religious doctrine rather than to a scientific ideology. This is considered ideology in that it requires a fair amount of faith in the original premises to accept the entire system. Such theories or ideologies are based on understanding rather than the kind of evidence demanded from medicine. Nevertheless, they may provide some clues as to the handling of the human aspects of severe psychiatric illnesses such as schizophrenia which may, in the end, prove to be organically determined. These ideas or concepts used by the curandero may not have scientific value in the same sense as do the psychoanalytic theories, but they have therapeutic value in that they help the curandero to arrange his ideas about a patient so that he can approach the patient in an integrated and organized way. By explaining the patient's problems and reducing the fearfulness of contacting the patient, the curandero can approach the patient in a therapeutic vein without being as frightened of the symptoms as others.

Mention should be made of the treatment setting, particularly because of its intrinsic therapeutic importance. Each curandero works in his own unique setting, depending usually upon his degree of affluence. The basic atmosphere created is invariably the same. In general, the curandero sees patients in a part of his home set aside for treatment. These rooms, even in poor slum homes, are distinctive because of the great number of religious objects contained in them. The presence of numerous pictures and statues of the Virgin Mary and Jesus, of various sized crosses and religious candles, which are often arranged around an altar in a corner of the room, creates an atmosphere of religious solemnity which makes one forget the poverty of the slum or the humble shack of the curandero. Indeed, in such treatment rooms one feels as if in a church, and cannot help but view the curandero with awe and respect.

The therapeutic effect of this "temple in the home" cannot be minimized. The quiet calm can invoke a feeling of security and protectiveness in the frightened and anxious. At the same time the religious symbolism can arouse the need for penitence and forgiveness in the guilt-ridden and "sinful." Perhaps most important is the authority the curandero derives through his relationship to the setting. It makes him the object of respect and awe and puts him in command of much of the power that derives from the patient's response to the setting and the symbolism. By relying upon religious symbols and objects that have great meaning for the patients, he can immediately establish himself as a man of wisdom and authority, which undoubtedy increases the patient's willingness to cooperate and his expectation of relief.

Once he determines the diagnosis through the lengthy interview, history-taking, and examination described above, the curandero has access to a variety of treatments. In uncomplicated cases, these are somato-empirical methods consisting of massage, decoctions to be drunk, and various rules of rest and diet, used alone or in combination. As disease syndromes become more complex and anxiety levels are raised he turns to a wide variety of magical and supernatural treatments.

Curtin, in an extensive study of the healing herbs of the upper Rio Grande, cited numerous illnesses for which the Mexican population had devised some form of treatment. (Curtin, 1947) While the present study did not attempt to gather the same data in great detail, an effort was made to check the curanderos' familiarity with these medicines. As expected, the curanderos knew and had used the great majority of the herbs described for essentially the same symptom complexes. Herbs utilized by this population demonstrate the extent of both their nosological considerations and their pharmacopoeia. The following, taken from Curtin, is a list of medicinal herbs and the conditions they treat: rattlesnake oil (*aceite de vibora*), rheumatism and snakebite; mineral water (*agua piedra*), kidney stones; garlic (*ajo*), diphtheria prevention, pain in the bowels, toothache, rabid dog bite, stomach trouble, snakebite; cottonwood (*alamo sauco*), swollen gums, ulcerated tooth; cottonwood (*alamo de hoja redondo*), boils, broken bones; sweet basil (*albaca*), hornet bite, colic, straying husbands; apricot (*albaricoque, hueso de*), dryness of nose, goiter; camphor (*alcanfor*), pain, rheumatism, headache, faintness; amaranth (*alegria*), heart trouble, tuberculosis, jaundice; alfalfa (*alfalfa*), keeps away bedbugs; filaree (*alfilferillo*), diuretic, rheumatism, gonorrhea; lavender (*alhucema*), phlegm, colic, vomiting, menopause; licorice (*yerba del lobo*), clotted blood; aster (*cosmose*), chest congestion, coupled with whooping cough; parsley (*anis*), painful shoulders, stomach troubles, colic; cocklebur (*cadillos*), diarrhea, rattlesnake bite; wild pitplant (*buchuheat*), pyorrhea, throat irritation, skin irritation; desert tea (*fir*), headaches, colds, fever, skin venereal disease, kidney pain, diuretic; scouring brush (*pingacion*), gonorrhea.

There are a number of treatments for viral upper respiratory infections. For *aire*, a term used to refer to an earache, stiff neck, cold, or dizziness and headache, the curandero uses a mixture of inhalation and sweating therapy. Stones are heated with various herbs in boiling water and the patient leans over the vapors. *Aire* means "breath" in Spanish. As one curandero put it,

> that means when a hot wind comes, happens like you are in a car and you get sick ; you get like seasick, you throw up. For some reason you feel it into your head ; the air gets into your body. I don't know how it gets there but it gets into your body somehow. For treatment, you get a black wasp and mash it and mix it with dirt. You can make little balls with the mud, and put it on the spot that hurts. You can also take a spider's web, and mix it up together. Then you put it in a glass of water and you let it settle down and you drink it, and that will settle you. I don't know if it's your nerves or what it is. I don't know why it helps. I guess whatever the dirt is, or whatever the dirt has in it, helps. After this you throw up.

For colds, teas, whiskey, and lemon juice with honey are drunk; liniments and poultices are prepared; or a lard-turpentine mixture, or paste of *chile* is put on the back of the patient. This leads to sweating. Rue leaves are sometimes stuffed in the nose or ears, or made into an infusion to be sniffed. For tuberculosis, tonics, herbs, and goat's milk are given. The treatment for rheumatic pains is hot sand or a heating pad which restore the heated part to normal temperature. For tonsillitis, one must rub his feet with Vicks Vaporub. Nosebleeds are believed to be due to overheating and are treated with a series of cold baths. A hot water bath with rosemary is the treatment for infertility, because the vapors warm the cold womb. Occasionally *osha* and salt water are used as an emetic. The root *inmortal* is occasionally ground into powder for upper respiratory infection, chest pain, fatigue, and tuberculosis. Spearmint (*yerba buena*) is good for female troubles, childbirth, the newborn, infant colic, and menstrual cramps. Cupping (*ventosa*) is good for muscle aches, and a liniment massage is good for the nerves. Massage distends and warms the nerves and is good for pain, joint pains, (*susto, empacho,* and *bolitas*) and lumps under skin.

There are, curiously enough, a minimum of herbs for the treatment of psychiatric conditions. This suggests that for such conditions manual restraint, confession, and other psychotherapeutic procedures were more common. *Yerba del dapo,* an herb in the aster family, is used for *saltido*, or jumping stomach, which appears to be a nervous kind of stomach disorder. A large ball made of the green plant wrapped in a cloth is placed on the navel to stop the throbbing. A number of herbs are also used as love charms to enhance performance and good fortune in the pursuit of love.

The curanderoes make decoctions and infusions of leaves, bark, roots, or flowers. Occasionally they mix the powdered form of the herb with oil and prepare salves, ointments, and poultices. While in some instances, specific curative properties are attributed to the drug or herb, they are often believed to be effective because of the association of prayers and magical rites performed when the herbs are given. As in other treatments, medicine is of value only if God wants the patient to get well.

Massage is used for painful limbs, sore back, and other musculo-skeletal disorders. Massage in the form of rubbing an egg over an individual's body is used for a number of anxiety syndromes and appears to have the effect of relaxing the patient. Nonspecific treatments, such as the sweat bath or vapor bath, which were quite common among the Spanish Indians of the Western hemisphere, are also used by the curandero.

Surgical procedures are not extensive, save for the bursting of blisters, incisions of abscesses, and the setting of fractures. No amputations or trephinations are done. Occasionally clitoridectomy is employed for the treatment of sexual *furor*. Cupping is used often in the treatment of colds, pneumonia, and other respiratory infections, as are applications of Ben-Gay or camphor and/or the use of vapor inhalations, although the explanation for the efficacy of such treatments has to do with concepts of *aire*.

While many of the above conditions are explained by folk concepts, they fall within the realm of natural illnesses and are treated empirically with naturalistic means. As symptom complexes become more vague and anxiety rises, magical conceptions are increasingly relied upon and treatment, while still empirical, takes on a less naturalistic quality. Thus illnesses caused by the magical intrusion of a foreign object into the victim's body are treated with somatic-empirical means. Whatever the real cause, treatment is designed to remove the foreign object believed responsible for the pain. One favourite method of the curandero is to rub the patient's body with an egg until the site of intrusion or painful area is identified. The egg is believed to absorb the intruding object or pain. Sometimes simple massage or cupping is successfully employed for the same reason. Sucking is rarely used. In cupping, a candle is applied to the site of the pain, and the lit end is put under a glass. As the encased air is consumed by the flame, a vacuum is created, causing the cup to stick to the skin. A welt often is raised as the "pain" disappears. Massage, heat, rubbing, and the infrequently used sucking have beneficial effects even though the concept of an "object," or more often *aire*, may not be a naturalistic one.

The treatments for *empacho* are remarkably similar and likewise vary to some extent from one curandero to the next. According to one Mexican-American mother:

> To treat it, you rub their stomach real good and rub them with an egg at room temperature, not from the fridge, and then you rub their stomach real good with it. Wherever that egg burst, that is where the *empacho* is in the stomach. Then they tie a piece of linen around to hold it there. After they do all the rubbing and applying of the egg, they give them a good dose of castor oil or something to make them move their bowels. Some kids seem to get *empacho* over and over again. They get it real easy. It doesn't happen to the kids whose parents worry about what they eat; it seems to happen to the kids whose parents don't care what they eat.

Another informant told a slightly different story:

> My little boy had it too. He was about a year old. Because he don't want to eat anything, and everything he eat, he spit it out, and they told me he had *empacho*. So I took him to a curandera. Well she turned the baby around and then she starts rubbing him like that. Until something breaks in the middle of the back. Yes, something snaps when he has got something there. She start working, working till it snaps. Then he starts feeling very good and all that. They know about it right away that he had *empacho*. My wife can tell. She starts worrying about him, he don't want to eat. She knows right away that he has *empacho*. She starts losing weight.

While cases of *caida de la mollera* can be treated in the home, they are frequently brought to the curandero, particularly when the family's anxiety is high. In all its essentials, the curandero's treatment corresponds to the family's. It involves turning the baby over on his heels, pushing up against the roof of the child's mouth, packing the fontanelle area with moist salt, and/or binding the area. However, there are variations. According to one curandero:

To treat it you push your tongue up against the top of the mouth or push it up with your hand in order to put it in place. It happens when older kids handle the little-bitty one. Until the hole disappears the baby is not alright and they worry about it. The child sometimes has [loose bowels] *correncia* with this, cries a lot, and is restless. Sometimes they run fever but it all depends on the child sometimes has loose bowels (*correncia*) with this, cries a lot, head, or put a patch on the space after you push it up from the inside. Sometimes you can put a chocolate plaster on, something to keep it sucked up, and keep the roof of the mouth in place. Sometimes you can fill your mouth with water and suck out the hole. Sometimes you put a ribbon in the hole, then you put a penny on the top of the ribbon and put a candle on top of the penny, then you put grease or shortening on top of the candle. You light it and put a crystal glass over it and that thing will make a suction and it will bring back the thing thats sunk. It is better for pain but I don't think it is too good for *mollera*, because it is hard to get it to stick up there. It is also good to say prayers for this such as Catholic prayers, *Ave Maria* and *Padre Nuestro* —three of each.

For *susto,* granada leaves are used.

Take the bush and rub it over the body. You doctor them every Wednesday, either at twelve noon or three o'clock in the afternoon. You get you a bunch of weeds, or herbs, and go over them like brushing them with these weeds. After that they come three different times a week and you pray. Recite a prayer in the name of the Father, Son, and Holy Ghost. Put a sheet of paper over the patient's face. Then throw water on the patient's face. This calms the nerves. This must be done at night when it is dark. If during the treatment the patient doesn't jump then he probably doesn't have *susto*. Occasionally massage with egg is good for *susto*.

The treatment of generalized anxiety as well as the more specific phobic anxiety of *susto* involves a combination of empirical remedies and magical maneuvers. One curandero advised that the "person with *nerviosa* needs tolerance from the people around—instead of shattering her to pieces, giving her support. *Niervos* are tiny elements radiating through the body which keep the balance. Any strain causes them to dry up and harden."

Patients are advised to take regular vacations, to listen to music, and to go on a regimen of "nerve softeners," such as vinegar and sugar with water. Nerve softeners are also good for hiccoughs and indigestion. Regular hot baths to open the pores, followed by cold baths to close them, are also recommended to allow the nerves to breathe.

For phobias, patients are advised to avoid people who remind them of their fears. They are also given one teaspoonful of sugar on their tongue, for the sugar is believed to seep down into the nerves of the neck, thereby producing relaxation. For violent behavior or epilepsy, the curandero takes two gallons of vinegar with 36 fresh figs, boils this to one gallon and one quart, and drains it. One teaspoon twice a day for 40 days is prescribed. This treatment is also good for *susto*. For *bilis* or anger, a tea is given.

To treat patients with pathological rage the curandero boils down a mixture of two gallons of vinegar with 36 fresh figs until one gallon and one quart remain. One teaspoon of this mixture is then taken twice a day for 40 days. Cannibalistic fantasies are attributed to "an enemy in the brain" and are treated by massage of the neck. This presumably keeps the spinal fluid from stopping up the head and leads to a gradual cessation of the symptom.

In the treatment of these anxiety disorders the curandero makes extensive use of confession. He follows the simple rule of getting the patient to tell as much as he can about the circumstances leading to the development of the difficulties. He may probe certain parts of this history for details, or remain silent when the patient speaks freely. His goals, however, are always the same. He is, first of all, interested in the history. More important, he is interested in getting the patient to reveal himself, to speak of that about which he cannot tell others. Thus patients are encouraged to tell of their transgressions, of their taboo violations, and of their weaknesses. "Stubborn" patients who remain mute are particularly difficult and much effort is expended in "breaking them down." Sometimes persuasion is used, with religious references. At other times, threats of punishment by God are used to get the patient to reveal himself, a technique which at times may account for critical remarks about the cruelty of curanderos.

According to the curandero, the confession is a particularly important part of the treatment of anxiety. It enables the patient to relieve himself of a troubled conscience, to share his worries and guilt with a comforting, supportive, helping person, and to gain reassurance about his fears. But more important, confession sets the stage for the treatment as a whole. Sometimes it is sufficient of itself to provide the necessary help. Even when it is not, it nevertheless is one of the key building blocks in the curandero's therapy. By revealing himself to the curandero, the patient entrusts himself to him and acknowledges both his dependency upon and faith in him, thereby establishing a state of mind which will be receptive to receiving help. For as the curandero repeatedly noted, it is necessary for the patient to have faith in him, if the treatments are to be succssful.

One curandero noted that essentially he inspires faith and confidence in the patient and is positive in his suggestions. At the same time, the patient must be willing to be healed, must be in a passive state or mood, and must have faith that he will be healed.

> By inspiring faith and confidence as to your ability to treat the patient successfully, you arouse hopes in the patient's conscious mind which in turn affects his subconscious mind. You gain the patient's cooperation by having him relax and remain passive in treatment. Never tell the patient he is not sick. Cite other cases so that the patient knows he is not the only one. Advise the patient not to talk with others about his illness since unkind suggestions by skeptics and unbelievers can reduce the value of the healer's suggestions. The time required for the cure is governed by the intensity of the patient's faith. The faith is purely unconscious and is gained by the conscious mind ceasing to object. The subconscious mind will accept all suggestions and it has absolute control of all functions, sensations, and conditions of the body. The healer must show the patient he has faith in himself and in his methods.

According to this curandero, the underlying techniques of psychological healing are, in effect, verbal suggestions from healer to patient, a combination of verbal suggestions with physical contact, which conveys magnetism, telepathy or thought transference, and auto-suggestion. The patient must be brought into a comfortable chair in a comfortable, partly darkened room, and asked to relax. After his symptoms are inquired about, he is encouraged to stop thinking of them, to close his eyes, and to think of nothing. No one is to be treated with his eyes open, which interferes with concentration. The patient may then be told of worse cases which the healer has cured until he is completely at ease. Suggestions dealing with each symptom are repeated eight or ten times, repetition being very important. Laying on of hands is an important aspect of faith healing and derives its authority from the Bible. Healing by hands involves passes over the pained site. No cures are instantaneous. Success depends on healer and patient, as in the use of suggestions.

Passivity in the patient is necessary. If a relative is necessary to keep the patient comfortable, he is allowed to stay. Relaxation of muscles is important, as is the healer's encouragement of the patient to like him. No interruptions should occur. The laying on of hands is useful for diseases but only suggestion is necessary if the problem is based only on bad habits.

The treatments of *ojo* and other folk syndromes are characterized by even more complex magical maneuvers, whose value can best be understood in terms of the nonspecific factors present in the treatment and in terms of certain hypothetical, psychodynamic explanations. (These are considered in detail in the next chapter.) While the use of empirical remedies, massage, cupping, prayers, and confession is similar in part to methods employed in Western medicine, the curandero's treatment of such folk syndromes as *ojo*, *embrujada*, and *envidia* is not, and as such is especially fascinating.

There are a variety of methods for treating *ojo*. One method has the person responsible for the *ojo* spray the child's face with water, following which both lie in bed together under covers. This may have some real value as it encourages sweating which, in the case of febrile illnesses, may be useful. If the person believed to be the source of *ojo* cannot be found, an individual named Juan or Juanita, after San Juan Bautisto, is sought to do the same thing. Another approach to diagnosis and treatment was described by one curandero:

> You have to break an egg and say a prayer. You break your egg, put it in the glass, and then put some little piece from the broom, you know, on top like a cross, and then the egg starts bubbling. You have to brush him with the egg first—make like a cross. The egg takes out the evil from the child and makes the person causing it stop. When he gets well, you know it's *ojo*. He start getting sad and his eyes get red and that's how you tell. He starts out like fever, you know, gets hot. That when somebody else look at a kid like that too much, and he don't touch it. He goes at home, starts crying, starts getting headaches, and you do that, with the egg, you know. When the egg starts boiling, that is when you know he had *ojo*. When the egg goes down, if it does not boil, it means that he doesn't have the *ojo*. All someone has to do, if they like the child is to go and touch it, you know, touch his eyes or something, you know. Don't touch it, that kid get sick.

In addition to somatic-empirical treatments, magical-religious treatments, including prayer and incantations, are employed. To help witchcraft victims, the curandero prays for the assistance of God and encourages the patient to confess his sins. He may also give the patient an amulet or charm, such as a crucifix, to ward off evil spirits and bring good luck. Various leaves, such as *osha* (parsley) and garlic, are often placed in small bags to be worn for preventive purposes about the neck. Sometimes herbs imbued with supernatural power through prayer are used in the making of decoctions.

When individuals have lost their souls to the devil, the goal of treatment is the recovery of the lost soul. By a careful inquiry into the events of the patient's life, the healer determines whether the patient has offended someone who may have retaliated by witchcraft, or whether the patient has turned from the ways of God, thereby losing his true Christian soul to the devil. Prayer, religious incantations, the wearing of charms, and other magical and religious efforts are utilized to get the support of God and to protect the individual from the devil.

The curandero often prepares, in plaster, clay, or cloth, a likeness of the part of the body believed to be affected by the illness. As he prays over the image, the harmful elements become absorbed by the imitation. This method is of especial interest because it is often part of more complex witchcraft techniques used by curanderos in the fight against sorcery. The procedure followed in counteracting sorcery is even more elaborate. First, to dominate the evil spirits, the curandero must be free from ordinary weakness and must be fortified by the grace and favor not of God, but of the satanic spirit world. The potential for evildoing requires the induction of a particular mental attitude through abstinence, prayer, ritual baths, and fasting, after the necessary prayers have been written on parchment. The curandero may fast for forty days prior to making the pact, since if he makes a pact with a full stomach, he may "go crazy," losing the strength to contain the power he obtains.

To perform black magic to counteract the *bruja*, the curandero must select the time of his act in relation to certain positions of the moon and stars that govern such things as the conjuring of spirits, necromancy, and the finding of stolen goods. A full moon is good for warlike, disruptive, and discordant acts, a quarter moon for destructive acts, and a barely visible moon for acts of death requiring invisibility. Next, the materials necessary for magic, such as a sharp knife, parchment, and candles are prepared.

Since blood sacrifices are essential for success in black magic, a lamb or other domestic animal is slain. This slaying insures the availability of fresh animal skin for the parchment on which the pact will be signed. The sacrifice ceremony is accompanied by detailed prayers, and the animal is killed with one stroke of a knife. The slain animal is removed and stretched; salt is added to it and it is then dried in the sun.

Black magic is rarely used. When it is, it is primarily for purposes of overcoming powerful witches, when other methods have failed. It is particularly resorted to following the evil seduction of an innocent young woman or unjustified harm to someone.

Religious measures are especially indicated when diseases are sent by others or arise through violation of taboos. Confession is central to religious forms of treatment and probably has a generalized effect through relief of guilt and anxiety. Religious therapy also includes purification, sacrifice, prayers, and atonement. Blowing is used, because God blew on the curandero when he was born, and it is a very sacred rite. By blowing on a patient during holy days and during baptism, the curandero can increase the patient's strength. Prayers are derived from Catholic liturgy, the psalms, the Kabbala, and various books of magic. Special prayers may be used for specific symptoms. For headaches, the patient prays directly to God for relief. He praises God for His ability to heal, and he may be anointed by the curandero. The patient with eye troubles repeats the same prayer seven times a day for three successive days, thinking always that God will help him. For prayer to be successful it is important that the patient genuinely believe in God and have faith that he will be helped. One curandero regularly wrote out a specific prayer or psalm from a "magic book" on a piece of paper which he gave to patients to wear around their necks. It was:

> Jehovah my Father, may it please Thee, for the sake of the great, mighty, holy, and adorable name, Jeschajah Baal Hatschna, that is Help is with the Lord (for he is the Lord of help—he can help) which name is contained in this psalm, heal me from my disease, infirmities, and from pain of my eyes, for this is the power and help and thou alone art mighty enough to help of this. I am certain and therefore I trust in thee. Amen, Selah.

When an enemy is suspected of causing the symptoms, the patient is instructed not only to pray to God for help but also to throw dust in the direction of the enemy or to pour water at the side of the enemy's residence or at some spot over which he will walk. Throughout, it is necessary to keep in mind that God will help. By thinking about the prayer and God and by dropping the water or casting dust, the suspicion and fear of the enemy soon disappear—faith is the curative.

Some people are advised to go to *Senora de Los Melagos*. There they can buy *miracles* (medals) or pins of the parts of the body, which, when placed on the satin apron around the statue of the Virgin Mary, are said to bring healing to painful parts. This particular chapel, which contains the oldest cross in San Antonio, is not qualified by the Church, just as the Society of the Virgin of the Guadalupe and the Society of the Blessed Virgin are not qualified as legitimate sites of miraculous cure. Nevertheless as the curandero said:

> People go there and get better because of the faith that they have in the cross. If you have strong faith, you will get well. If you don't have strong faith, you won't. Then you will die or be crippled. If you believe hard enough on anything you will get better. Thoughts have power. If you think something hard enough, it comes true.

The treatment of *envidia* and *embrujada* involves various combinations of religion and supernaturalism. According to the curandero, *envidia* may sometimes be treated at home although it is preferable to:

> turn evil to the evil, which is to the devil, or to make a special novena nine nights or nine mornings. It is good to pray to a certain saint to show you a way out. You don't want to think bad about your enemies, or if it's evil that has been put on you, you want to pray to the Church.

According to one Mexican-American woman, if she believed someone put a spell on her, she "would have to find a curandero."

> Oh he would probably adjust you, you know and tie up some contract with this person [the evil-doer] like a lawyer would tie up another case. They all have to agree. If one doesn't agree, that's it. The curandero make you a picture of the person that caused the trouble in the beginning and they reverse the charges, in other

words. It's something like electricity—it's the spirit of the person
who did that thing got more than the other one. You get it just
when you try to take more than your share and you feel guilty.

The treatment of *embrujada* is often more difficult than that of
envidia. A young married man described his wife's experiences in
being treated for *embrujada* in the following way:

> She went to see that woman [curandera] over there, you know ;
> she went and told that somebody, that they don't like her. Yes,
> she know that they don't like her, and they do something to her.
> It affect her inside and all that, you know, and the pain inside.
> And from there she had a nervous breakdown. I took her to a lady
> [curandera] over there and she told me that she has got to go to
> the mental hospital and keep her there for two weeks. That's all
> she last there, about two weeks. She was fixing something in the
> house, I took her two chickens, and they were going to fight
> together, you know. And she did something else, I don't know.
> Oh, she put something on the house so it won't happen again.
> Like she put two cans of those, what you call it, like lime or
> something, she put two, one in the front and one in the back.
> Well she told me to take them off in about two or three months ;
> that would take everything from there. She know that they don't
> like her, you know. Because she started getting sick and all that
> and that lady told me the next day that she don't like her. Well
> she told me to move, but I had to sell the house. She told me that
> it was from the next-door neighbor. She don't like her because
> we had property and all that. And I had a good car, I had a good
> job. I think thats what they don't like, you know. I lost my job
> on account of that too. The same thing affect her, I feel nervous,
> I lost my job. About three months I had no job. I went to that lady.
> All she told me to drink some kind of water, I don't know. She
> gave me some kind of water and some kind of herb. I boiled it
> and then I drink it for about ten days. I was going into a nervous
> breakdown myself. Yes. She burn all my clothes. But she never
> bother the kids. She burn all my clothes and broke everything
> inside the house. Everyday. She started hollering and crying.
> That's when she started getting sick. Well, she said a lot of things,
> a lot of bad things. Like sob, and all that, you know, like crazy.
> Yes. On me. She don't like me because I think that lady was try-

ing to make me take a divorce. Right. She throw me out of the
house, scratch me, all that. That lady told me that she was trying to divorce me from her too. I was getting the same thing, but
I never got that far. She got me, all right. She had some shock
treatments over there at the state hospital. And the doctor told
me that it was the same thing happen as the lady. She charge
about fifty dollars for six times. She pray and all that. She was
about fifty-five or sixty. She lives on Cincinnati St. I knew her
from some other neighbors, they sent me over there. She told me,
"It cost you fifty dollars," and I pay her fifty dollars. Yes. It was
worth it. She has got plenty of things in there, dolls and, you know,
like little soldiers and all that. She spend a lot of money because
she has got to go to Mexico and bring something from over there
and come back. You know, we just paying expenses. That what
she told me: "I have to charge fifty dollars because I have to go
over to Monterrey, come back, and you can give me anything
beside that you want" But she just wants the expenses she spends
going and coming back. Go and bring some of those weeds and
all that. No, she can't get them here. She has to buy it over there.
Well, no, she got to have some help. She can't do it by herself.
I put those two cans, and she told me that that lady won't bother
me no more. I see her, and all that, say good morning to the old
man. I knew that they were the ones, you know. Because she told
me. I wouldn't have suspected anything. I don't know where it
come from. They have been living there for a long time. The lady
[curandera] say if you want to get better you have to move from
that house, sell it, do something. So I sold the house. Now I am
living all right, living a good life now. She told me it won't happen
to me no more. My wife feels all right. She told me she could do
the same thing to her. Her got a big business, got a drive-in. She
told me I could break that too. Put him out of the house too. I
told her no, I don't want to do that to them. Let God do it to
them. Yes, she could have done it, she told me. I don't know how
she would work it, I think she would work the same thing that she
was doing. But she told me another colored guy was doing that.
He took about two months to do it. He was working and working every day, working every day, doing something, throwing on
the yard, you know, they throw something on the yard. How it
started, how it was. She had a little chapel and she was reading a
Bible or something there. It a little hard to take it away, because
he works for two months. I took her over there, and she told me

your wife is going to have another breakdown. So you have to take her first over there. Anyway I put her for two weeks over there. Give it two weeks and then she will be out of there. So I had to go see her first. Yes, everybody living here. Yes, they knew that she was doing all that. They told me, "I told you that lady don't like me." I see her son and all that, you know. And they told me. It was not their fault, you know, that their mother was doing that to us. We say, "Well, that's all right." They tell me its not our fault. Not their fault that their mother was doing that to us. I told them I had been out of a job just on account of your mother. I lose my job, put my wife in the hospital, take care of the kids. It all your mother's blame. Well, don't blame us, we do nothing to that. Because she don't like us. On account of, like I told you, I had a good job. No. She tells what happened to you. Like she told me, "I going to get you a job." She says, "I want to give you a job and you go to Lackland. They hiring people over there and before you go inside, say a prayer and they hire you right away." That's how I got this job, the first job. Yes, she told me. She told me don't you worry. I get you a job. Any kind of prayer that comes to you. All the lady want is for me to divorce her, you know, and lose everything. The neighbor, she want me to lose everything, divorce her. Yes. She told me. She says you can't do that. Right. Because of the neighbor. Well, something was coming up on me too, you know, I was getting crazy and I said I was going to get a divorce and see if I change. She said, no, we are going to stay together. It is not on you and your wife. It's this lady that is doing all that to you, getting tired and all that. So now we are together and living a good life. But I had to move from there.

In this man's description of his wife's treatment can be seen the great value the curandero places on thoughts, on the magic of words, and on faith. The patient and her husband are given certain activities by which they can express their aggression. At the same time, they are encouraged to have faith. The underlying mechanisms are several. One is clearly suggestion. More important, perhaps, is the attempt to preoccupy the patient with a required task that clearly takes his mind off his worries. A further factor is the reliance on prayer, which is one of the first methods of anxiety-reduction learned in this culture. It clearly has a specific effect in comforting the patient. Special prayers for insanity or melancholy are regularly repeated by the patient and the curandero. A prayer is also recited over a pitcher of well water which is then used to bathe the patient. One prayer, which is said several times during the bath, asks God to restore the senses to the patient who has been plagued by the devil. Another method for casting out an evil spirit involves mixing a specific number of leaves in a pot, which is prayed over and exposed to the open air for twenty-four hours, at which time it is poured at the door of the patient.

Occasionally special prayers are written on tree bark or paper, folded, and placed around the patient's neck. The patient is thus given a meaningful and complex ritualistic activity in which to engage and is encouraged to concentrate on some special word or prayer which leads to a lessening of his concentration on his problem. He is also encouraged to think in terms of improvement and is supported in a situation where he quite naturally expects to improve. The suggestive influence of the healer in this situation would appear to be enhanced by his use of generally accepted and mysterious religious forces, which are brought into play through the power of prayer. In addition to prayers, such things as the casting of water on the path of an enemy and the wearing of a protective amulet provide defenses against anxiety, a sense of reassurance, and outlets for emotional expression.

Related to kabbalistic use of prayers, psalms, and secret names is interest in the magical qualities of numbers and their significance in predicting the future. Names and numbers are separated into two divisions. The first is concerned with the meaning of individual numbers and the second, with the practical application of the numbers to names. Thus, the number one is thought to be a strong, active, masculine number which represents individuality, strength and boldness. The individual who is a "one" tends to be self-centered and to see everything in terms of himself, refusing to utilize his senses to appreciate other people or other things. Such individuals are often officious and dominating. Number two is considered to be a feminine, peace-loving number, and is thought to be the ideal number for mothers, doctors, and nurses. Charm, endearment, affection, and attachment are words that describe number two. This list goes on and on. The healer may attempt to demonstrate that the patient's name and number correspond to traits different from those he imagines he has, thereby encouraging him to feel more comfortable about himself. In addition, numbers enable the person's problems and traits to be attributed to something other than himself, which relieves anxiety.

Patients are expected to return regularly to the curandero to report on how well they adhered to the requirements of treatment, such as saying the proper prayers at the proper times. Nonadherence is thus a potential source of anxiety for patients who are fearful of displeasing the curandero. With the development of such a transference relationship to the healer, the patient often displaces anxiety from its original object onto the curandero. With this approach to treatment, patients gain relief from their anxieties through the support given them by the curandero and at the same time gain confidence by assuming some responsibility for their own problems.

The curandero does not guarantee instant success, but makes healing conditional on the individual's reliance on God and on the healer. Prayer thus helps to reduce anxiety and also contributes to the patient's gradual independence. The healer also recognizes that some individuals want to remain sick, so as to dominate their families and remain free of responsibilities, and are not truly motivated for treatment. The wise curandero recognizes that he cannot help such patients.

As one intelligent curandero said:

Each man must carve his own destiny. Those who fail lack faith in God. With faith, which is a quality of the healthy mind, man can accomplish miracles. As Jesus said, "To Him that Believeth, all things are possible." Thought has power and can be constructive or destructive. As Jesus said: "As a man thinketh in his heart, so is he." The greatest power in the universe is the power of suggestion. It is the real cause of mental healing and is influential through the subconscious mind, the seat of the soul, and the emotions. Faith is the second greatest force in the world.

VIII

The Therapeutic Value of Curanderismo

CURANDERISMO PERSISTS in the American Southwest because it works. Before considering some of its specific and nonspecific therapeutic elements, some of the more general reasons for its perpetuation in a modern industrial society should be noted. Of great significance is the fact that the social-cultural milieu for Mexican-Americans is very much as it was for Mexicans. The perpetuation of traditional laws and values has been due in part to the proximity to Mexico and the relative ease with which ties with the "old country" can be maintained. These factors have discouraged Mexicans from fully participating in the American social system, both in terms of the positive rewards associated with adhering to traditional ways and in terms of the negative sanctions against breaking with tradition. Furthermore, the positive rewards of American life have been denied to the Mexican-Americans, who have encountered prejudice, discrimination, and limited opportunities for both vertical and horizontal social mobility. As Mannheim pointed out, only when horizontal mobility (geographical) is accompanied by intensive vertical mobility (between strata), is the belief in the general and eternal validity of one's own thought forms shaken. Since the Mexican-American has not participated fully in the American social system, he has not questioned his own world view and has not fully explored the validity of the American world view, save for adopting in large measure the negative, derogatory, and stereotyped view of himself that has arisen from prejudice. Inasmuch as traditional forms continue, curanderismo persists among those who have not become imbued with the American way of life.

Another factor contributing to the stability of the traditional folk beliefs and practices of curanderismo is the authoritarian structure of Mexican family, social, and religious life, for such a structure supports the status quo and the persistence of traditional social, religious, and medical practices. Whatever the strengths of such a system, it is certainly more likely to persist when alternative forms are less accessible, such as is the case of the Mexican-Americans who are not readily accepted into the mainstream of American life. The young learn early to accept both the authority and the wisdom of their parents and their Church and are not rewarded for independent questioning or for challenging authority. The world is a given, not an object for manipulation, change, or mastery, as it is for those raised in accordance with the Protestant work ethic. Individuals cannot reject ideas and beliefs without rejecting the authority of others. Such a pattern of rejection is discouraged for it can create enormous psychological conflicts, as seen in the case of *inglesados*. The Church reinforces this attitude of unquestioning acceptance by rewarding passive acceptance and adherence to obligation. Such a background unwittingly prepares people for an uncritical acceptance and faith in folk medicine, even when they are given the alternative of modern medicine.

In an earlier volume, *Magic, Faith, and Healing*, papers were presented based on research in a variety of cultural settings, that focused on the beliefs and practices of various primitive groups with regard to psychiatric illness. Attempts were made to describe the prevailing beliefs about the origins of psychiatric illnesses and to describe techniques for their treatment. Furthermore, an attempt was made to understand the common psychotherapeutic elements present in the techniques used in these diverse primitive psychiatries and in contemporary psychotherapy. All instances included a specific set of techniques designed to allay anxiety and relieve fear, a group experience designed to reintegrate the patient into the fellowship of his tribe, and a set of beliefs which made understandable the distressing experience of the illness and the relationship of the patient's previous experience to it and to the particular aspects of the therapeutic process.

These techniques which ranged from animal sacrifices and possession states to the ingestion of pharmachologically active substances, all served to increase the patient's susceptibility to suggestion and to increase the prestige and power of the healer in the eyes of the congregants and the patient. The increased susceptibility was enhanced by the anxiety of the patient and by the techniques themselves.

The patient comes to treatment with a certain loss of confidence in his customary ways of behaving. His habitual responses are no longer appropriate. Somehow or other there has been a failure in adaptation. The patient is increasingly anxious and increasingly dependent upon the situation to provide him with cues in terms of how he should behave, to advise him of what to do, and to reassure him about what is happening. Factors in the treatment techniques contribute further to the patient's anxiety and sometimes even induce fear in him. Among these factors are admonishment by the healers, spirit possessions, and animal sacrifice. Feelings of guilt and shame may also be generated by the public confession of sins and taboo violations. Alterations in mood and a reduction in consciousness and inhibitions were also generated by combinations of alcohol, drugs, self-flagellation, music, dance, starvation, and fatigue. The increased susceptibility appeared to be enhanced by the production of alterations in mood and/or consciousness of the patient, ranging from complete unconsciousness, as in the possession states to mild alteration in body perception, physical sensation, and temporal orientation, and the production of euphoria, as in some of the less dramatic treatment maneuvers. The alteration of mood and/or consciousness contributed not only to a reduction of recently acquired neurotic responses, but to an examination of specified factors in the patient or in the situation which were said to have produced this altered state of being, i.e., an increased suggestibility.

Perhaps the most prominent distinction between prescientific psychotherapeutic techniques and contemporary psychotherapies is this emphasis on the production of a dissociative or emotionally charged state in the patient. However, in many cultures this occurs in a subtle and undramatic way, where the crux of the method is in the interpersonal interaction of the healer and patient, with less reliance on additional techniques to produce alterations in mood and consciousness.

Many nonspecific elements in treatment contribute to its value. The curandero provides a body of empirical knowledge concerning emotional illness and abnormal behavior and a means of controlling it that serves his group, much as other systems of medicine serve other groups. Much of what the curandero does is magic, in that his maneuvers are often not rational and have little objective value. Malinowski defined magic as follows:

> We have seen that all the instincts and emotions, all practical activities, lead man into impasses where gaps in his knowledge and the limitations of his early power of observation and reason betray him at the crucial moment. The human organism reacts to this in spontaneous outbursts in which rudimentary modes of behavior and rudimentary beliefs in their efficiency are engendered. Magic fixes upon these beliefs and rudimentary rites and standardizes them into permanent traditional forms. (Malinowski, 1948, p. 82)

Certainly the curandero's approach fits this definition more than it does Radcliffe-Brown's, which stressed the symbolic adherence of the performer to certain traditionally expected observances, where society expects the individual to be anxious. Often the failure to perform a ritual or to adhere to certain taboos is associated with anxiety and the development of psychic stress. In this regard, it is of interest to note that in Mexican-American culture, as in many others, illness is tied up at times with various kinds of sexual behavior, such as incest, perversion, homosexuality, autoerotism, bestiality, and aggressive behavior such as homicide, cruelty, theft, insult, ridicule. The disease situation serves certain social purposes, for both the patient and the group are reminded of the importance of adhering to the cultural prescriptions. This is especially well demonstrated by the curandero's treatment of those individuals who have made unsuccessful attempts to become acculturated to American society. Illness serves to re-establish these individuals in the Mexican group when they have broken away from traditions. Someone who suffers from a folk illness like *susto* will be excused for his neglect of Mexican ways and will be accepted back into the group by undergoing folk therapy. Traditional treatment serves also to defend traditional Mexican ways by attributing certain illnesses to the American way of life. By seeking traditional treatment, the group focuses attention on the value of Mexican culture and leads to a reaffirmation of group loyalties and traditions.

The curandero manipulates the patient's anxiety and guilt about the violation of cultural taboos by using a variety of culturally meaningful symbols and techniques. He takes advantage of the fact that almost everyone has something to be guilty about or ashamed of in order to generate the patient's involvement in the treatment and thus bring about a cathartic, supportive experience. By relieving the feelings of guilt which he may have induced, he relieves the anxiety associated with the illness. It is not necessary to focus on the specific anxieties the patient brings to treatment, since he creates in the patient anxiety relative to the treatment and also redefines the patient's anxiety in terms of culturally meaningful treatment. The central element in the treatment is the relief of the induced anxiety. The patient's anxiety is thus superseded by the anxiety and other feelings which the curandero has induced and which he manipulates in his treatment.

The operation of these factors is well illustrated by the method of confession used by the curandero. This method is especially valuable in relieving guilt and anxiety. Confession to the curandero is a dramatic and significant event, since it enables individuals to express feelings which are ordinarily not permitted expression in his culture, the effect being further enhanced by the often public nature of the confession. Confession not only emphasizes the importance of adhering to group rituals, but has many features of a shaming maneuver. This relates to the use of shaming in child training and, no doubt, to the inclination among both children and adults to deceive one another, as a way of circumventing the rigidity of status and role demands and the great stress on outer form and self-control.

The magical-religious orientation of the curandero provides an integrated and meaningful view of both inner and outer experiences, both for the believer and the patient. As Mannheim has noted:

> From whatever source we get our meanings, whether they be true or false, they have a certain psychological-sociological function, namely to fix the attention of those men who wish to do something in common upon a certain "definition of the situation." (Mannheim, 1936, p. 21)

Thus, by virtue of defining a given syndrome of behavior and anxiety in a certain way, the curandero sets up a distinguishable social situation from which derive certain positive or therapeutic, restorative maneuvers. Much as illness must be considered an integral part of the "motivational economy" of the social system, as Parsons has suggested, so too therapy must also be treated as part of the motivational balance of the social system. Therapy involves restoration of the individual to a position where he can function in his social roles.

In addition to the usual etiological factors producing illness, illness develops in situations where strains are imposed on the individual, with which he cannot cope. These strains center at two main points, the individual's acceptance by the group in an appropriate role and his upholding of the value patterns of the group. In that illness is one way of dealing with strain, it shares many of the features of social roles. Thus, the "sick" person and the group relate to each other in relation to a set of norms defining expectations of appropriate behavior in this role. Since the sick person is exempt from the performance of certain normal social obligations, his claims to sickness must be socially defined and validated. The sick person is also not held responsible for his own state and is expected either to get well spontaneously or to get cured. He cannot just decide to get well. He and the group must accept his condition and then unconsciously deal with the underlying motives. That the patient is not responsible is partly supported by the numerous projective devices present in the folk culture.

The price paid for exemption from ordinary responsibilities is the fact that the sick role is socially undesirable and this should be ended as quickly as possible. Furthermore, the sick person is isolated from many desirable normal functions. Since being sick is defined as being in need of help, the patient is obligated to cooperate with the healer, which exposes him to specific reintegrative forces, the motivational processes of which are the opposite of the motivational aspects of pathogenesis. In treatment, the patient is accepted as a member of a social group and receives unconditional support from the healer, who is permissive and accepting and encourages him to express ordinarily repressed wishes and fantasies. While normal sanctions of disapproval are suspended, at least on the verbal, gestural, and magical level, the curandero does not reciprocate the expectations of the patient's deviant wishes in that he does not interact with him as others have. In that he controls his own responses to the patient's behavior, he is better able to bring an end to the vicious circle of increasing symptomatology brought about by the group's over-reaction to the patient. Furthermore, the curandero is in a position to give and withhold approval because of his prestige and reputation and because of the nature of his relationship with the patient. Adoption of the sick role is a ncessary antecedent to a re-examination of patterns of living gone awry and a preliminary step toward reintegration of the individual into the community and re-establishment of a previous harmony.

Curanderismo shares many of these nonspecific features not only with other forms of folk psychiatry but also with contemporary psychotherapy. The benefits obtained from folk treatments and contemporary dynamic psychotherapies derive, in large measure, from elements such as the patient's expectation of relief from a culturally designated healer using culturally meaningful procedures and powerful symbols, the arousal of faith, and the inducement of suggestion.

In addition to these general therapeutic features of curanderismo that can be found in other therapies, there are a number of specific factors meaningful only in terms of this culture. Successful treatment appears to require within each context specific, culture-bound factors such as a shared assumptive world of beliefs and attitudes of the healer and the patient and a responsiveness on the part of the healer to the subtle psychological needs of patients within his culture.

These specific factors make sense when we consider that curanderismo derives from the shared needs of the members of the group; these needs have developed from similar cultural experiences. The Mexican-Americans—as all other people—must contend with certain universal anxiety situations. How these situations are handled will depend upon the traditional and characteristic ways of handling anxieties in the culture. It appears likely that what gets defined as a source of anxiety and the ways for dealing with the anxiety will be learned early in an individual's life and will appear in certain specified patterns of socialization, characteristic psychological conflicts, and general values shared by the members of the society. Taking this further, it is likely that the universal anxiety situations will lead to the arousal of these latent anxieties which, in turn, will color the meaning of the universal situations, and that such anxieties will characteristically lead to the use of traditional methods for handling the original anxieties. Varying with the orientation and characteristic experiences in cultures, there will be

Curanderismo

certain situations which are probably culture-specific in producing anxiety and which, too, will lead to the use of traditional methods of anxiety-reduction. Related to this is the fact that certain beliefs in themselves may serve as sources of anxiety even though they are initially used to explain other anxiety-provoking experiences.

We have looked closely at the problem of mental illness with the idea of demonstrating the interrelationship between characteristic personality traits and psychological conflicts in this particular subculture, and the characteristic psychological defenses and group-designated procedures (defenses) for handling anxiety and conflict that are used by both the mentally ill and the healers. We have found that Mexican-American culture creates characteristic psychological conflicts and characteristic patterns or defenses for handling these conflicts. Furthermore, we have found that the ways Mexican-Americans handle anxiety—which, in exaggerated form, are seen in so-called mental illness—are, in form and content specific for this culture, and, indeed, that the kinds of defenses chosen are also selected from a wide range of possible defenses on the basis of the experience in this culture and the emphasis given to certain kinds of defenses over others. That is to say, there is a Mexican way of being mentally ill, and it is difficult to recognize some of its syndromes, relative to our own nomenclature. We have found that the system of folk psychiatry developed in this culture is an extension of the psychological defense maneuvers employed by normal individuals and that treatment maneuvers are in fact attempts to deal in a more complex and emotionally powerful way with the anxieties that individuals cannot handle alone. This system of psychiatry, like the individual patterns of defenses, is related to characteristic personality patterns developed in this society and also is weighed heavily in the direction of the kinds of psychological conflicts more likely to develop in this society. This relationship is seen both in terms of the problem areas that are given the most attention by the curandero and in terms of the therapeutic maneuvers employed by him.

Our material shows that curanderismo has developed not *de*

novo, or by simple accretion, but because of its integral relationship to the kinds of problems encountered by Mexican-Americans and because of its relationship to the kinds of defenses and values characteristic of them. One major form of anxiety for Mexican-Americans, as for all groups, is illness and insanity, or abnormal behavior. How the curandero deals with it has been seen to relate to how he views the situation, the characteristic Mexican-American ways of handling anxieties, and the state of empirical or scientific knowledge of the group. Curanderismo is also related to the characteristic beliefs and values of the group. Looking more closely at mental illness, we have seen that mental symptoms are defensive measures against psychological conflicts and anxiety. We have also seen that individuals can handle anxiety in ways typical in the culture, or in personal ways. That is to say, a person can develop patterns of symptoms in line with defenses characteristic for members of his culture, or he can become sick in his own way, which may have little resemblance to the conventional patterns of illness. When the latter sickness occurs, it is likely that the individual is more deeply disturbed and as such less able to rely upon convenient, culturally shared beliefs and patterns of behavior both to express and contain his anxiety.

Psychiatric concepts, beliefs, and methods are similarly related to earlier learned methods of anxiety-reduction and to the particular kinds of unconscious personality behavior and fantasy patterns that develop in the Mexican-American family and culture. Curanderismo is not only based on empirical observation and necessity for handling the problem of the mentally ill, but it is intrinsically related to the basic assumptive, perceptual, and cognitive world of the members of this culture. For this reason, cultural explanations about sources of illness are acceptable to individuals from this culture. For this reason also, treatments are useful in resolving the basic personality pattern and conflicts of this group, even though such concepts and methods are not based on scientific theory.

Looking at the curandero's therapy from a psychodynamic viewpoint, we can see a number of other subtle, intricate operations. In

157

treatment, the curandero attempts to clarify the patient's problem both for himself and for the patient, but does not assume that a cure is dependent upon insight nor upon the resolution of a conflict established early in the patient's life. He focuses primarily on manipulating the "here and now" and is fundamentally concerned with symptomatic relief.

A real cure of a psychoneurosis, according to strict psychoanalytic criteria, requires a solution of the hypothesized original childhood conflict, so that the original motives of the neurotic defense or symptom cease to exist and the warded-off instinct is expressed in a mature, sublimated way, through displacement of its energy onto other nonobjectionable strivings. Since, according to psychoanalytic theory, the neurotic defense or symptom is by definition inaccessible to reasonable judgment, the original motives and warded-off instincts cannot be altered or redirected unless they are brought to consciousness by a technique, such as psychoanalysis, specially designed to do this.

Resolution of neurotic conflicts in the psychoanalytic sense is unlikely to occur with the methods of the curandero, but its unlikeliness is no reason to reject the validity of his methods, which have developed over time to deal with the particular needs of Mexican and Mexican-American patients. Indeed the curandero's methods would appear to be more appropriate for the people he treats than would a more psychoanalytically oriented approach. Mexican-Americans are, in general, fearful of authority and conform to social norms because of external controls on their behavior, rather than because of internal controls. For them, the acceptance and reassurance of an authority figure such as the curandero is very forceful in influencing changes in their attitudes and behavior. Such reassurance may have limited value if the anxiety that motivated the original repression is very great. However, even in these instances where the presenting problem represents the remobilization of old conflicts, the positive transference toward the therapist may help overcome the conflict.

The curandero is usually able to alleviate the factors contributing to the clinical exacerbation of symptoms, thereby bringing relief. Relief is possible because neuroses that derive from a conflict between instinctual impulses and the suppressive forces of the society can be modified by an authority figure who, at the same time that he represents the social forces of the group, permits a limited expression of these blocked instincts. The model for such treatment is confession, where the patient can admit desires, wishes, fantasies, and taboo violations to the accepting curandero. Confession is especially valuable for individuals reared in a society where external control of behavior through shame has been the preferred method of socialization and social control.

For traumatic neuroses and acute anxieties associated with life crises, the curandero provides an opportunity for belated discharge of excitation associated with fear and anger, as well as rest, reassurance, and suggestion. By verbalizing his feelings, the patient may be helped to see better the reality situation and to gain control over irrational tendencies to react. Patients can face verbalized ideas better than unclear emotional sensations. Through persuasion and reassurance, the curandero can help individuals to accept a changed reality situation, and by supporting passive needs and dependency longings, he helps fight tendencies toward regression. With magical operations, gratification of wishes and fantasies are also provided. Various physiological methods, such as warm baths, may relax the tense patient.

While psychodynamically oriented psychiatrists work to undo underlying neurotic symptoms, the curandero strives to increase the defenses against anxiety by his use of persuasion and suggestion. Some even approach patients in a critical and reproachful way, which is effective in increasing the repression of the conflict, since patients are often fearful of disappointing the curandero. The patient must pray to get support from God (which will in itself be anxiety-reducing) and to avoid arousing the curandero's anger, which might prevent improvement. The repressed conflicts are expressed in treatment in terms of dependency upon the curandero, creating effectively a substitute neurosis. This is to be contrasted with more psychoanalytically oriented therapies, where the undoing of the repression enables the repressed infantile strivings to participate in the growth of the personality. The curandero allows only partial discharge of affect and instinct, creates a dependency relationship, and insures that the rest of the repressed strivings will remain so. The folk beliefs that are used to explain the patient's difficulties provide a form of insight into his problem and also serve to reinforce the repression of conflict for individuals experiencing either early or late symptoms of schizophrenia. Folk beliefs and practices offer culturally acceptable explanations for strange happenings within and around the patient. They thus have value in reducing anxiety and in maintaining contact between the patient and the community.

Certain of the curandero's procedures provide substitute symptoms. Exercises, baths, and other physical measures provide gratification for physical impulses less directly expressed in the symptoms associated with *susto* and *embrujada*. Similarly, prohibitions serve as artificial phobias. The fear-ridden patient can focus on thoughts (suggested by the curandero) of nonthreatening, albeit tabooed, activities and ideas, the avoidance of which is connected with the idea of cure. Exact advice as to diet, and curative rituals such as prayers, penances, and magical formulae in a similar way act as artificial compulsions, while baths have a purgative and atoning effect.

In addition to the above benefits, the relationship with the curandero recreates the passive-dependency relationship of childhood, providing the patient with a sense of security and protection. The religious aspect of the treatment also serves as an atoning ritual which, according to Fenichel, renders a neurosis superfluous. The innumerable medications and herbs to be taken counteract the "bad stuff" inside and therefore serve as a kind of artificial paranoia. The effectiveness of the therapy then lies in the fact that it offers all things to all patients, thereby satisfying the components of the psychological conflicts presented by different patients.

The curandero's role in the society undoubtedly contributes to his therapeutic effectiveness, since strong transference feelings usually develop toward him. He is very powerful and is believed to be omniscient, and thus arouses much respect and fear. At the same time he is viewed as being apart from the group—odd, different, and perhaps even "crazy," which suggests that there are certain unconscious hostile feelings toward him, especially when anxiety is not high and there is no need of his services. The curandero thus is a reincarnation of the infantile view of the all-powerful parent. This view is reinforced by the fact that he is a source of love and protection at the same time as he is the object of unrealistic castration fears.

In a culture where great emphasis is placed upon castration threats, the curandero can promote the repression of the symptoms that are derivatives of the original repressed impulses. Conversely, when the curandero is reassuring, the patient may give up his symptoms in the hope of obtaining love and appreciation.

According to psychoanalytic theory, transference improvements are not trustworthy ones, for they do not undo the pathogenic conflicts of childhood but simply displace and repeat them. That they displace them is partly because improvement turns on the patient's dependency on the curandero, not on any real "working through" of the pathological conflicts. In this dependency, the patient reverts to passive-receptive mastery as in the first years of life when omnipotent others care for him. The curandero relies on conditional authoritarian methods in that he says that only if the patient is a good "child" will he get what he wants, i.e., love and protection. Neurotics in the Mexican group, as elsewhere, are always looking for passive-dependent protection. According to Fenichel: "The more a psychotherapist [or curandero] gives the impression of having magical powers, of being the representative of God, the more he meets the longing of the patients for magical help." (Fenichel, 1955, p. 253) Certainly in this culture which permits and encourages magic, such an approach will prove of value.

The material examined in an earlier section suggests that the individual in this culture is prepared very early in life to accept the kind of treatment the curandero can offer. In the family setting, the individual learns concepts of authority and formal relations, religion, folk beliefs, and superstitions. Much learning takes place on a less conscious level as well, contributing to the emotional sources of behavior and personality—the fantasies, myths, and magical thinking—and to the mental productions of disturbed individuals who have difficulty in keeping emotional conflicts hidden.

The study of these personality patterns yields clues to the individuals' unconscious and to what Devereux has called the "ethnic unconscious" of the members of a given subculture. Such study also helps us to understand the value of traditional folk medical beliefs described in this book and some of the reasons for their persistence. The characteristic Mexican way of thinking and of behaving in relationship to others is not a chance thing, but is due to the persistence in each member of the group of certain emotionally significant and shared fantasies, formed early in life.

In much the same way that specific speech is learned by selective reinforcement from the many sounds made by the human infant, characteristics and emotional patterns or emotional languages are learned by the reinforcement of certain patterns and the non-reinforcement of others. In their early life, Mexican children encounter certain similar problems and attitudes because of similarities in the personalities of significant adults in this culture. It is because of similar attitudes, beliefs and values about good behavior for children that children develop certain shared feeling patterns and emotional attitudes, which underlie and determine their future reactions to events and people.

A dominant theme among men is self-control and the ability to keep things to oneself. While *machismo* seems to be a conscious ideal, it is, when considered with the other patterns, such as the Don Juan complex and the attitude toward woman, a clue to unconscious themes that cannot be directly expressed in this culture. They must be expressed in other ways, such as in the form of a folk illness or in folk treatment.

162

While women are highly regarded as mothers and wives, they are looked upon as potentially unfaithful and untrustworthy, which may partly account for the fact that they are heavily watched or chaperoned. Even women sought after as sexual objects are considered as potentially dangerous. This threatening aspect of women finds institutional expression in the curandero's acknowledgment of beliefs about witches and black magic. Viewing these beliefs as projections leads one to the inference that women are unconsciously feared. This makes sense when one considers the traditional over-protectiveness of the Mexican mother who infantilizes her children and who at the same time desires to be viewed as devoted and loyal. Such experiences clearly lead to much repressed hostility toward mothers which cannot be expressed openly, but can be expressed indirectly in projections about dangerous witches and temptresses.

The paradoxical view of women is further understandable when one considers that the young Mexican-American child is exposed to a protective mother who, because of her own earlier experiences and often because of the grandmother and surrogate parent system, may view the child as a sibling rival and treat him accordingly. Since traditional role obligations not only prevent the open expression of resentment towards mothers and older sisters, but also may require placing them on a pedestal, the inhibition of sexual and aggressive drives toward women naturally follows. This inhibition leads to the institutional separation of affectionate and sexual objects, as in marriage and prostitution, respectively, and in the institutionalization of aggressive drives through various projective systems.

In this group, the pattern of mothering, which consists of generous demand breast feeding for the first two years of life, leads to the development of certain basic emotional attitudes in the children. Babies, while developing a sense of importance from being able to obtain their satisfactions at will, are also likely to develop an unconscious fear that the overworked mother may one day reject their demands and perhaps even retaliate by biting and eating them as they have her. The child who is deprived earlier may manifest rage and anger and appear troubled, but obtains, paradoxically, at the same time, continual reassurance by the fact of his mother's continued love.

Excessive indulgence encourages unrealistic expectations of continued gratification of dependency needs. These expectations may lead in adulthood to unrealistic optimism and magical thinking. At the same time, aggressive fantasies and fears of retaliation remain rudimentary and unmodified by the experience of minor deprivations until the age of two to three. These fears may be nurtured by the mother's shift from affectionate indulgence to indifference and aloofness in the presence of a domineering mother-in-law, and may be intensified during weaning or when the child is displaced by another sibling, an experience for which he may be unprepared and which may occur simultaneously with exposure to new demands of child training. This abrupt discontinuity relates to the distrust of others, which finds institutional expression in the widely held view that one must guard oneself against others and keep thoughts and feelings to oneself to avoid being taken advantage of by others. At the age of three, the ever-present mother is no longer available; her absence contributes to the child's sense of impotence at suddenly being denied the experience of omnipotence and indulgence. It is no doubt partly because of such experiences that mother figures remain in fantasy as both dangerous *brujas* and all-loving Virgins, representing both the repressed hostilities toward the rejecting mother and the unsatisfied longings for the pleasant, bygone dependency. If the child cannot turn to an all-accepting mother, he may turn to the Virgin for acceptance and favors.

The father remains at a distance during the upbringing of the child and is both the rival and the major source of authority. The rejected father, who himself identifies with the child and feels rejected by the mother's attention to the child, has hostilities which sometimes appear in his cruel treatment of his children. The characteristic resolution in this culture of the male child's relationship to his father is his identification with certain of the superficial patterns of masculinity he sees in the father. The Mexican boy's unconditional adherence to the father's demands is manifested later on in the Mexican unconditional acceptance of the curandero as an authority figure; this acceptance also enables him to recapture the passive-dependent state of childhood. Passivity yields help and assistance and sometimes fulfills the childhood expectations of competence. In the religious sphere, individuals admit to helplessness at the hands of God and fate, a pattern which is particularly apparent in illness and which is invariably utilized by the curandero.

Much as mistrust of the universe may stem from the uncertainty in relationship to the mother, which we have noted above, a paranoid trend may develop from a son's intense Oedipal rivalry with his father. The son must assume a passive relationship with the father, even during late adolescence, a pattern which can lead only to the repression of any positive feelings toward the father. Nothing permits the recognition by either the father or the son of tender feelings. There thus remains a residue of emotional need for a male figure, which can be very threatening, in view of the rigid demands made on masculinity. Such needs are satisfactorily fulfilled by male support provided by the curandero, but in other relationships where individuals must deny such feelings or desires, paranoid mechanisms are often used. The individual converts his feeling of love to one of hate which, since it too cannot be expressed, is projected onto male figures who are seen as victimizing him.

It is likely that a preoccupation with food and a belief in magic relate also to these early experiences. Both food and magic can be good and bad and both are sources of evil and illness. Fears of poisoning or of various vapors entering the body are also important, and are meaningful projections of the original experiences of the incorporation of love and hate from the loving one and the ambivalent feeling concerning this. One positive result of this early indulgence is seen in the emphasis in treatment upon oral elements such as herbs, magical prayers, magical words, and supplication. Other positive results are also reflected in other facets of life: beliefs and rituals are not precise, concern for time is negligible, and the incompletion of tasks is not a source of discomfort.

Because of difficulties in identification with male figures, the fear of not being a man is a problem for many. This fear may account for the frequency and seriousness of accusations of homosexuality, which invariably result in violence and other culturally defined expressions of masculinity. Preoccupation with impotence and loss of virility, which shows obvious castration fears, is common and relates to the pattern of relations between men and women. Young men are encouraged to seek out prostitutes and often boast about such exploits, which provides a superficial source of anxiety-reduction in the area of sex. The prostitute plays a not unnecessary role in this subculture, for she affords a return to the early stage of receiving unconditional acceptance. Masculinity is thus demonstrated by recourse to an older woman or a woman of easy virtue, both of whom may give unconditional acceptance and restore the individual to an earlier state of infantile omnipotence. The patterns, however, are clearly ones in which passive-dependent needs are simultaneously being gratified, making such sexuality pregenital in kind.

At the same time and in much the same way, the women are expected to be modest and self-effacing. Mexican men show an inclination to be somewhat narcissistic and exhibitionistic and indeed are expected to exhibit courage, daring, and sexual prowess. Such characteristics, Jones has suggested, are elements of the God Complex and appear to derive from the oral stage. (Jones, 1923) This belief is supported by the persistence of certain elements of oral pessimism in the Mexican personality, such as finding pleasure in the anticipation of calamity and disappointment; and in developing a defensive kind of courage, as in *machismo,* which appears in anticipation of anything which would threaten autonomy and independence (which are, in fact, impossible to achieve in this culture). An exaggerated sense of self-control serves to keep individuals unaware of unfulfilled dependency needs as well as unresolved Oedipal fears. Supporting passivity and fatalism is the fact that children are taught how insignificant and powerless man is in the presence of God and in the hands of fate. This view is reconcilable with the authoritarian tenor of father-child relations, when one sees how parental behavior itself is a reaction formation to parental feelings of inadequacy although they rationalize inadequacies in terms of religious doctrines and beliefs about fate. The counterpart of the authoritarian Mexican male is the submissive Mexican female, whose masochism has been made into a virtue. That Mexican women accept domination and an ostensibly inferior status to men is rationalized in terms of loyalty or love.

Because of strict upbringing in a system that fosters belief in magic and folk illnesses and because of the perpetuation of certain kinds of infantile interpersonal relationships, the Mexican grows up with much fear about his own emotions, particularly hostile and sexual ones, as well as much fear of the things that arouse his emotions. One way of dealing with these fears is to retreat from the world of action to the world of words, which no doubt accounts for the unusual verbal ability of even the most illiterate peasant. According to psychoanalytic theory, the first words of childhood have a magical and omnipotent quality and are dynamically related to the use of blessings and curses, which in adult life are expressions of the same kind of word thinking. For many Mexicans, thinking and talking are substitutes for emotions and carry much more meaning and effect than they do for Americans. Thoughts and words are powerful and can be used to kill and to cure, and they retain for adults much of the omnipotence they have for children. The prohibition on action tends to invest thoughts with much feeling and increases acceptance of the belief that thoughts can influence matter or reality. It is for this reason that words and thoughts are considered critical aspects of the curandero's treatment. According to Fenichel, the tendency to use omnipotent words as a defense against danger explains the fact that secondary defensive measures against compulsive symptoms often have the compulsive form of worded magical formulae. This is seen in the curandero's high regard for and frequent use of magical words and prayer.

In addition to defensive patterns acquired by the solution of socialization problems, other patterns develop at later stages as solutions to both earlier and later problems. These appear in the unconscious contents of obsessive doubts and relate especially to questions of masculinity *vs.* femininity, love *vs.* hate, and id *vs.* superego. The Mexican emphasis on self-control, conservatism, the present, and formality in interpersonal relations all act as defenses against the omnipotence of thoughts and associated guilt feelings.

Fenichel believes that "most patriarchal religions also veer between submission to a paternal figure and rebellion, and every god, like a compulsive superego, promises protection on condition of submission." (Fenichel, 1945, p. 302) The anxious or depressed Mexican patient who has grown up in a patriarchal system against which he cannot rebel deals with this ambivalence by strict adherence to the compulsive ritualism offered him by the curandero's treatment methods. Further suggesting the presence of unresolved guilt about rebellion and hostility toward parents is the great emphasis on superstition, oracles, and rites, especially for those who fear the magical effect of the words of others. When an individual consults a curandero to find out about the future, he is, in a psychodynamic sense, seeking either permission or forgiveness for something ordinarily prohibited or he is attempting to shift the responsibility for his guilt onto the curandero. This is also the mechanism in the confession to the curandero. Guilt feelings are also allayed by making charms which serve either to undo the guilt or to deny its presence and the danger of punishment.

Since many emotions aroused in this culture are not expressed, many individuals feel guilty much of the time. Indeed, the less opportunity for expression, the more likely it is that thoughts of bad things will arouse the same guilt that would have been aroused by the act. Charms are useful in relieving guilt about evil thoughts. One basic conflict in Mexican personality, then, is the defense against the Oedipus complex, which cannot be successfully resolved by the means provided by the culture. Castration threats are traumatically presented at early ages, and they lead to a fixation at an early level of pregenital organization, probably the anal-sadistic level. This assumption is supported by the presence of other compulsive-neurotic traits in the defense hierarchy of Mexicans, such as reaction formation, undoing, isolation, and an over-cathexis of concepts and words. Thus the Mexican contends with a harsh super-ego through self-punitive and expiatory symptoms and through treatment experiences which tend to satisfy the needs of this superego.

In the anxiety disorders of *susto* and *mal ojo*, internal, instinctual dangers are projected onto external dangers. Since the expression of impulses is forbidden, there is a tendency to utilize such mechanisms as projection and displacement, which dissociate the individual from his affective experiences. Such projections as are seen in *susto, ojo, embrujada,* and *enviada* are attempts to escape from dangerous internal impulses by avoiding external situations that symbolically represent the impulse. Thus, *mal ojo* is an escape from guilt and aggressive impulses aroused in parents by illness in a child, while *susto* is an escape from anxiety and perhaps sexual impulses. Two recent anthropological studies lend support to our theories that internally experienced anxiety created in certain situations is handled in a culture-specific way through folk illnesses. This follows from the theory that people learn not only socially acceptable ways of "going crazy," but also a hierarchy of culturally sanctioned defenses that are reinforced by the beliefs and attitudes of others. In *caida de la mollera*, the mother becomes anxious that her child might have fallen when the child is inattentive, has diarrhea and fever, or is crying and restless. Since a mother is criticized if her child is sick or harmed through neglect, it is not unreasonable that mothers become anxious and seek to explain the child's problem and their distress in a culturally meaningful way. Illness in a child also causes hostility toward the child, on whom the mother is dependent for her status and toward whom she may also have many unconscious hostile feelings. Labeling the child's problem as *caida* enables the real or imagined blame to be focused away from the mother. At the same time she has opportunity to relieve her guilt by following certain culturally prescribed patterns. If the illness is more severe, the child older and the mother more dependent, the same situation may be labeled differently. Thus, according to Rubel, an *empachado* condition often arises when an individual (usually a child or guest) is made to eat against his will. (Rubel, 1960) In such a situation a child may be caught between not wanting to be disrespectful to his mother and wanting at the same time to be independent. According to Rubel, while *mal ojo* and *susto* are caused by stressful interpersonal relations, *empacho* may be due to the nature of a role relationship in which the prescribed behavior of one individual is that of unresisting compliance to the will of another, as in the case of a child and his parent or a guest and his host. *Ojo* and *caida* also result from having feelings incompatible with prescribed role behavior, since mothers cannot have feelings other than maternal ones toward their children. Rubel has described several cases of *mal ojo* that were believed to be caused by an unusual amount of attention having been paid to a child by a person whose relationship to the child did not permit such familiarity, that is, by someone outside the family group. Similarly, *susto* occurs when a man is embarrassed or greatly harassed by his wife, who reverses the sex roles by making him the passive partner.

Susto is of interest from another point of view. It is a form of phobic anxiety and depression manifested usually by symptoms of depression, anxiety and withdrawal from normal social activity and responsibility. *Susto* is believed due to a sudden fright, which leads to the soul's escape from the body. (Gillin, 1948) The treatment is designed to recapture the soul and return it to the patient. Close observation of the syndrome suggests that *susto* is actually an explanation brought into play after an individual has become sick. *Susto* is, in this sense, a culturally meaningful anxiety hysteria syndrome that affords the sick the opportunity of being recognized. While in anxiety neurosis an inner tension exists as free-floating anxiety or readiness for anxiety, the anxiety in anxiety hysteria is specifically connected with a special situation that represents the neurotic conflict or that reactivates the unresolved early conflict which cannot be handled by customary defenses. The instinctual situation may bring fear of castration or loss of love. Although the phobic person, as in *susto,* primarily flees from a threatening environment, he is in reality in flight from his own impulses to commit an aggressive or sexual act. Projection also serves as a way of guilt reduction. Thus, fear of external objects replaces fear of conscience; this replacement is reasonable in a society where fear of punishment by external authorities has already been learned in relationship to the Church.

The inclination to rely on projective and phobic mechanisms in this culture is promoted by a socialization experience that encourages the dependent child to think of himself as omnipotent and at the same time to fear his own impulses. The individual learns that thoughts are powerful, that his impulses are bad, and that he is not responsible for his own sources of gratification and self-esteem, nor for his own behavior. This kind of experience leads in varying degrees to a favoring of phobic and paranoid defensive or adaptive mechanisms and to both the explanations of illness and the content of illness found in this group. This experience also relates to the curandero's treatment approach, which appears to be of particular benefit for patients with phobic obsessional paranoid symptoms such as are found in *mal ojo* and *susto* (phobic), and in *embrujada* (paranoid-obsessional).

Looking more closely at the tie-in of treatment with the phobic paranoid element in these folk illnesses, one notes that the curandero provides the specific thing that such conflicts require for their resolution. Common to these folk illnesses is a regression of thought and feeling to stages seen in childhood, when dangers could be overcome by finding protection at the hands of omnipotent objects in the world. The *embrujada* or *susto* patient who fears his impulses or punishment for his impulses tries to regain that favorable childhood situation. All *embrujada* and *susto* patients behave like children whose anxieties are soothed by maternal protection and support. Such demands for reassurance by parent surrogates is common among phobics and paranoid patients and such reassurance is the major maneuver applied by the curandero.

The return of the person who made the evil eye and who represents not only the protecting parent but also the unconsciously hated parent also allows for some resolution of the conflict. He is first an object of unconsciously projected hostility and he then becomes the source of projected hostility. Further suggesting the ambivalence toward such a person is the fact that he or she must return to give reassurance and love—thus providing maternal satisfaction and support as well as the reassurance that no harm has come to him. In *mal ojo*, certain unconscious conflicts relating to the expression of hostility are projected onto innocent individuals in a culturally sanctioned way. Since those accused of causing *ojo* are frequently intruders into the home, this hostility may also represent hostility toward the intruder which cannot be expressed because of the need to maintain formal, correct, and hospitable relations with others. The stranger may perhaps upset the balance at home, since everyone must behave kindly toward each other while he is present. This may increase their resentment of him. Parents may also feel guilty about their own repressed hostility toward the child, which they are made aware of when someone expresses niceties toward their children. It is of interest that treatment of *ojo* often involves not only the curandero but also the stranger who has caused the illness as well.

The presence of the person causing the *mal ojo* in the treatment serves the further purpose of diverting the patient's mind from unconscious fantasies to reality by reassuring him that he has not killed this person. This is important, since the original impulse for the *mal ojo* came from the victim, who felt he was being made sick, or, in cases of children, from the parent of the victim. The sick person and the person accused of causing *mal ojo* are not consciously aware of their feelings. Since everyone in the culture has an unconscious reservoir of hostility, each is readily willing to admit he is responsible for the *mal ojo* and, since each feels uncomfortable about having such hostile feelings which are clearly aroused by the accusation that he has caused the trouble, each is willing to return and participate in the treatment.

The dynamics are more complicated when children suffer *mal ojo*. Here, the parents' hostility toward the child is projected onto the individual believed to have caused the illness. When a child becomes sick with an unexplained fever, fear regarding its health arouses unconscious fantasies of its death, which must be dealt with by projection onto others, preferably strangers. Often individuals may be selected because hostility toward them already exists, because of their success, their sensuality, or whatever it is they have that represents a threat to the group.

This view is further supported by the psychoanalytic notion that a morbid fear for the well-being of another conceals an unconscious hatred, and it is this feeling from which the other person must be protected. This view is also seen in the over-protectiveness of Mexican mothers, for their attitude would appear to represent both a denial of repressed hostilities toward their children and an indirect expression of hostility.

An additional element in *ojo* is the individual's fear that his own impulses may lead to the harm of another, either the child, or the stranger. This element is translated into the phobic concern for self expressed by the *ojo* victim or parent. In psychodynamic terms, this concern is a self-punitive identification with the unconsciously hated object.

One of the gains of phobic symptoms, as in *susto* or *mal ojo,* is the satisfaction of dependency needs—which is ordinarily denied to Mexican men. Although women are not expected to be independent, they, too, frequently have unfulfilled dependency needs, due in part to lack of attention from their husbands and, earlier, from their parents. When individuals crave the dependency gratifications of childhood in fantasy, they must also face the unpleasant insecurity and fears of childhood, which tend, in general, to reintensify their anxiety.

Recognizing that the fear of developing *susto* and *mal ojo* leads often to an avoidance of certain special situations and to an avoidance of expressing certain feelings, the curandero's treatment often involves exposure of the patient to the feared experiences; this experience serves to bring the neurotic conflict into the open. Having present the person who is believed to have caused *mal ojo* reassures the patient that this person has not been harmed by his projected unconscious hostility and that there is nothing to fear. Contact between the patient and the "perpetrator" of the evil eye further reduces the fear and mystery of the idea that harm will occur.

Thus the healing principles contain elements dovetailing with typical ethnic conflicts and needs, especially the passive-dependent needs and the need for mastery of internal aggression. The accumulated aggression is handled through reinforcement of the projections, displacement, and concretization. The villager who suffers from *susto* believes that he is being frightened by external forces (ghosts). He expects cure from the curandero, who reinforces the belief that the ghosts have taken hold of him. The next step is dependence on the curandero's attributed power to deal with the ghosts. When the curandero provides the patient with images to destroy and leads the patient to express his aggressive feelings and fears, aggression and fear are displaced to objects on a fantasy level. As Frank has written: "The patient's expectation of help is aroused partly by the healer's personal attributes, but more by his paraphernalia, which gains its power from its culturally determined symbolic meaning." (Frank, 1961, p. 62)

The fatalistic, passive-dependent expectation is seen in the slum dweller's attitudes toward God, parental figures, shrines, and curanderos. The curandero's role is actually connected with this aspect of the individual's psychology. Again, Frank has said: "The core of the effectiveness of methods of religious and magical healing seem to lie in their ability to arouse hope by capitalizing on the patient's dependency on others." (Frank, 1961, p. 62)

IX

Conclusion: The Relative Merits of Curanderismo and Dynamic Psychotherapy

IN THIS BOOK we have examined the wide-ranging impact of Mexican culture on personality, beliefs, and practices. We have seen how from birth onward, a person's biological functions are molded to culturally prescribed limits and patterned after accepted models accounting, no doubt, for shared attitudes found among people from the same culture. Thus, autonomy, initiative, and aggression, although suppressed early in the life of Mexican-Americans, are ultimately expressed by projection onto unseen malevolent agents in the culturally sanctioned areas of sorcery and magic. In the same way, cultural sanctions encourage the development of certain behavior patterns and attitudes that would be considered unusual in Protestant, Western society, such as the subservience of women, the freedom of men to engage in extramarital affairs, and so forth.

Cultural factors also influence the patterning of sick roles, which at times may serve to satisfy needs no longer being met through conventional channels. As Madsen has shown, by falling sick in a traditionally Mexican way, the Mexican-American is relieved from the responsibility for forgetting his origins. Being ill with *susto* may restore the anxious and conflict-ridden individual to the good grace of the community through reaffirmation of traditional Mexican patterns and family solidarity. Similarly, because of changes in the structure of the family, the male must assert his masculinity in patterns of deviance such as can be seen in adolescent gangs. Although this behavior is associated with violation of the law, it expresses previously valued elements of willfulness and courage. Here the instinctual drives that were idealized and sanctioned in the past create conflicts and are expressed in self-destructive ways, in contrast to the restitutive functions such factors play in the development of folk illnesses.

Culture also seems to influence the forms of illness and the kinds of treatment developed to deal with them. It is for this reason that many of the treatment methods fit so neatly the needs of the patients with these disorders. That is to say, folk psychiatry can be defined as the culture-specific methods of anxiety reduction using universally valid strategies and techniques for the treatment of what appear to be culture specific psychiatric disorders.

Worth noting, too, is the emphasis among Mexican-Americans on the larger social significance of illness, which contrasts strongly with its reduced social significance in American society. Because illness often suggests that something is wrong in the family, the sickness of a single individual arouses collective fear and family action.

In the Western world, by contrast, medicine has become increasingly secularized, and, as Ackerknecht has observed, "has lost its 'sacred' character, its social control function, its subjective influence on society, its meaning in moral terms." (Ackerknecht, 1958) The effect of such secularization can be seen in the hospital experiences of patients who, as Simmons and Wolff have noted:

are classified according to their illnesses, fitted into a tightly organized and scheduled system of hospital practices, and pressed into lines of conformity that are new and disturbing. Then in their emergencies they are cut off measurably from the tried and trusted contacts and supports of family and community. Indeed in the patient's darkest hours, physically, mentally, and emotionally he is likely to feel, and perhaps also to be left, rather much alone, especially if these periods come at night. (Simmons and Wolff, 1954, p. 177)

To Western man, illness is an impersonal event brought about by neutral, nonemotional, natural agents, such as germs, while for the Mexican-American, illness relates to an individual's life, his community, his interpersonal relationships and, above all, to his God. In such a culture, illness is a social as well as a biological fact. Because of its central significance illness is clearly related to other beliefs and patterns in this culture. Disease is defined not only in naturalistic, empirical, symptomatic terms, but also in magical and religious terms. In the same way, diagnosis and treatment occur in the larger, more meaningful context of major institutions and belief systems, not isolated from them, as in the United States.

The previous chapter has underlined nonspecific factors universally found in systems of medicine, as well as factors specific for curanderismo. A consideration of the ways in which curanderismo differs from contemporary dynamic psychotherapy further helps to underline the culture-specific nature of this treatment, and sheds new light on certain aspects of dynamic psychiatry.

The curandero's treatment clearly lacks the kind of depth probing and orientation toward insight and basic personality change that are the goals of intensive, psychodynamic psychotherapy. The curandero does not meet the criteria of scientific impartiality that Boyer has outlined for the psychoanalyst who maintains a scientific attitude. The psychoanalyst does not substitute logic for evidence, offers interpretations only as working hypotheses to be tested against further data, and expects his patient to preserve and utilize actively an observing segment of the ego.* (Boyer, 1964)

Thus the curandero does not avoid the chance to exploit the patient's uncritical worship of him in the therapeutic process; he is unlike the analyst who, according to Kubie, "knows that the patient's effort to look upon him as omniscient and omnipotent is a symptom of the patient's neurosis, a direct carry-over from infancy," which must be broken down to make therapeutic results lasting. (Kubie, 1950, p. 145)

While the curandero encourages passivity and sometimes total submission in the patient, the dynamic therapist encourages the patient to take increased responsibility. The curandero subtly and consciously encourages complete faith in his system of thought and his personal qualifications and total submission to his directives, and rewards emotional enthusiasm. He subtly induces regressive ego states in his patients in his attempts to get at symptoms and consciously binds the patient to him, thereby strengthening the false notion that he himself is omniscient and omnipotent.

By contrast, in psychoanalysis, according to Boyer: "effort is made not to bind the patient to the analyst or to his fantasies about the analyst but rather to clarify such fantasies and thus enable the subject to progress steadily toward greater freedom from the influences of his unconscious conflicts and the immature forms of logic used by his unconscious." (Boyer, 1964, p. 412)

* Recent studies have challenged this notion of the objectivity of psychotherapy and have indicated that suggestive factors operate even in psychoanalytic therapy (in which there is presumably the least active participation by the therapist). The dreams of patients and their reports of improvement often conform predictably to the theoretical expectations of their psychoanalysts, and the patients often show shifts in values toward those of their therapists. (Fisher, 1953) That therapists unwittingly influence the verbal behavior of patients by faint cues of approval or disapproval has also been demonstrated during interviews, and it is likely that they may influence patients' thoughts outside therapy sessions as well. (Rogers, 1942) Thus suggestion, reassurance, and direct influence may play a bigger role in rational psychotherapies than is ordinarily recognized.

In addition, the curandero has as his goal the relief of symptoms and distress. The dynamic psychiatrist views symptoms as defenses against underlying pathological conflicts which must be brought to the surface and overcome if any true, lasting benefit is to come. More specifically, dynamic psychotherapy, which has been greatly influenced by psychoanalysis, differs from curanderismo in having as one of its major goals a change in the patient through the growth of his insight into the nature of his difficulties. An attempt is made to assist the patient to see the influences of unconscious attitudes, processes, and feelings on the pattern of his daily life, in his inter-personal relationships and, most important, in the transference aspects of therapy.

These considerations suggest that whereas curanderismo sets great store in the traditional absolutes, faith and obedience, dynamic psychotherapy strives for objectivity, impartiality, and a search for scientific evidence. While criticism of curanderismo as unscientific "faith healing" is implicit in these distinctions, this is not my intention. Indeed, the study of curanderismo questions specific techniques, philosophies, and goals of contemporary dynamic psychotherapy, which may have developed more for their compatibility with the ethos and value system of our own culture than for any well-founded scientific reason.

A sense of fatalism, an adherence to traditional ways, an acceptance of a mystical non rational view of the world, an emphasis on form and *dignidad* and a reluctance to accept personal responsibility are all central values and assumptions of Mexican-American culture that are contrary to those emphasized by psychotherapy.

Contemporary psychotherapies, which adhere in practice to the existentalist dictum that "existence precedes essence," place great emphasis on the objective nonmoralizing examination of the patient's faults in the presence of the therapist. Mexican-Americans, by contrast, place great weight on safeguarding the inner worth, dignity, honor, and value of the individual. This makes them reluc-tant to discuss their feelings with others and makes psychotherapeutic engagement difficult. This reticence also finds expression in the idealized image of *machismo,* where self-restraint and self-reliance are considered critical parts of masculinity. At the same time, Mexicans only trust those with whom they feel an intimate personal relationship, a relationship which is difficult to establish with the psychiatrist. An aspect of this is the over-idealized evaluation of mother and father in this culture, an evaluation which makes it difficult for a patient to talk about his mother and father objectively.

The rapid development and acceptance of psychotherapy in American society have often been linked to American optimism and faith in personal and social progress through change. The Mexican-American, who is more fatalistic and accepting of his lot, is not initially as receptive to the goals of psychotherapy. The Mexican-American attitude has usually been one of heroic defiance of or passive resignation to fate, in contrast to the trust in reason and the mastery of nature which has characterized the Americans. The Mexican-American is often willing to accept fluctuating states of health and the vagaries of life as inevitable or as the will of God, not as a difficulty within him which requires personal change. Individuals from this culture are not often obsessed with a sense of guilt at not proving their worth, a common motivation for psychotherapy among Americans.

The minimal stress on individual responsibility is reflected not only in the major role of religious rituals and symbolisms in the culture, but also in other vivid belief systems relating to the presence of many such phenomena as *mal ojo* and *susto.* Coming from a culture that strongly supports projective mechanisms, patients who are prone to see all evil outside themselves quite naturally find the basic premises of psychotherapy difficult to accept, since these premises seek the source of difficulties within the patient.

According to Frank, the high value placed on democracy and science in America is reflected in the theory and practice of psychotherapy. The democratic ideal is made up of such values as personal betterment and freedom from the tyranny of tradition. It accounts in part for the public's acceptance of such values of psychiatry as self-betterment, freedom from inhibition, and a certain degree of independence of thought and action. At the same time, the scientific ideal reinforces the democratic ideal by rejecting dogmatism and upholding objectivity and intellectual comprehension, which, as Frank has suggested, may not be entirely advantageous for psychotherapy. Such an orientation results in an overevaluation of the cognitive aspects of psychotherapy, an undue stress on the niceties of interpretation and an avoidance of therapeutically valuable emotion-arousing techniques like group rituals, dramatic activities, and direct influence of the physician. In keeping with the Protestant ethic, great emphasis is placed on patient participation or "work" in therapy, the extent of progress being the responsibility of the patient. Egalitarian values are operative in the psychotherapist's avoidance of the traditional authoritarianism and direct influence of the physician.

At the same time, it should be noted that dynamic psychotherapy contains many nonspecific aspects found in other forms of treatment. Even the emphasis on a "scientific approach" has symbolic value in our society, and impresses the patient with the importance of the techniques of the psychiatrist. The psychiatrist's familiarity with a specific procedure and theory of personality adds further to his prestige. The technique of the contemporary psychiatrist also serves to increase the patient's susceptibility to accepting his "belief" system. The psychiatrist creates a sense of awe about himself by his knowledgibility and use of "scientific" symbols and procedures. He also induces anxiety in the patient by not responding to the patient in accordance with the patient's expectations of interpersonal relationships or of relationships to a psychotherapist. In addition, a review of emotionally charged areas may increase the patient's guilt and shame and add to the emotional shakeup so crucial for increasing his susceptibility to change.

The development of insight is the therapeutic goal in dynamic psychotherapy and serves to relate apparently meaningless or unassociated factors in the patient's life, so that he has a better understanding of the nature of his problems and the nature of his experiences. This insight, which makes less mysterious what is going on within the patient, also serves to increase emotional susceptibility by startling the patient. The use of intellectual formulations in treatment has value as an appeal to a more abstract authority, when the authority of the psychotherapist is no longer enhanced by the cultural context in which it occurs. It is thus possible to examine insight not from the viewpoint of its validity but from the viewpoint of its place in the psychic economy of the patient.

As in prescientific or folk psychiatries, anxiety disrupts confidence in the patient's conventional or traditional ways of handling things and increases his dependency upon the current situation and upon the psychiatrist. The disruption of the patient's assumptive world is followed by affirmation of the beliefs of the psychiatrist. Participation in an unconventional relationship that tends to challenge normal cognitive and emotional controls oftentimes generates a fear of losing control and a resistance to the procedure. The feeling of losing control leads to a sense of helplessness, which can be seen not only in the regressed psychoanalytic patient but also in more primitive therapies in individuals possessed by spirits. Body-image and perceptual distortions also may occur in the course of intensive psychotherapy, much as they occur in those entering possession states.

The absence of traditional patterns of relating, patterns which ordinarily contribute to a sense of identification, may disrupt the patient's sense of identity and self-esteem and lead to a loss of confidence in past patterns and habitual responses to life. Guilt and anxiety with regard to his failure to adapt to the therapy situation may challenge the patient's sense of autonomy and initiative and make him increasingly dependent upon the therapists as to what to do, how to behave, what to consider as right and wrong, and so on. This dependency may bring some temporary security, although the therapist may again challenge the patient's newly acquired viewpoint, thus setting in motion further uncertainty and further search for the problem.

Characteristics about himself which the patient holds valuable and worthwhile may not be valued in the therapy situation. Indeed, much of what may have been positive may become part of a temporary negative sense of identity, bringing dissatisfaction and low self-esteem. These feelings may contribute to marked anxiety. The very process which enables the individual to reduce his anxiety in the therapy paradoxically ties the individual to the therapist. This would be maladaptive if it were not for the fact that the therapist recognizes this adaptation and challenges it.

The patient gradually comes to see his behavior, comes to understand some of his unrealistic motivations, and tries to change his pattern of behavior. This process is, as I have suggested, not easy and oftentimes for patients who are not too strong, it is very upsetting.

Examination of our material thus far suggests that there are many similarities between curanderismo and contemporary psychotherapy and that many of the differences are due not to scientific factors but to cultural ones. A definitive study of the essentials of psycho-therapeutic processes and a definitive assessment of the therapeutic values of specific forms of treatment have, however, yet to be done. Despite a concern for scientific method among psychiatric investigators and theorists, there is little evidence forthcoming to prove that dynamic psychotherapy in its application meets the kind of criteria demanded by the physical and biological sciences. There is also little evidence that the value of dynamic psychotherapy increases proportionately to an increase in its scientific nature, which might strengthen the view that it is of more value than folk systems of treatment.

Finally, there is no evidence that dynamic psychotherapy is of more value than such forms of treatment as curanderismo. In view of this it is not unreasonable to speculate further about what appears to be the relative merits of dynamic psychotherapy and curanderismo for the treatment of the great range of psychiatric disorders. These considerations would be unnecessary and superfluous if evidence were available indicating that dynamic psychotherapy was more valuable than curanderismo. Given that it is not available, then, such considerations have special merit and value in enabling us to examine these therapies, and especially contemporary psychotherapy, from a new and wider perspective.

A consideration of the relative merits of these two treatment approaches could be formulated by asking whether curanderismo is more appropriate for treating psychiatric disorders than the psychotherapy model, and, more specifically, which if any disorders is it more appropriate for treating.

For purposes of discussion we may conveniently group psychiatric disorders into three categories. First, there are those with specified etiology for which there are specific treatments. These are the organic psychoses caused by infectious agents (syphilis), nutritional deficiencies, toxic substances, and degenerative processes. Included here too would be the inherited disorders such as the mental deficiencies, some of which (phenylketonuria, mongolism) are now preventable or controllable. The prescientific nature of curanderismo is most apparent when one considers it in relationship to this group of disorders. The curandero is not the equal of his modern counterpart when it comes to making an adequate differential diagnosis on the basis of etiological knowledge. He cannot distinguish the effect of general paresis from pellagra psychoses, nor is he skilled in the early diagnosis and treatment of tuberculosis, meningitis, and epidemic encephalitis. Similarly, he is ill-equipped to conceptualize the subtle distinctions among the various agents known to affect psychological functioning through direct damage to the central nervous system, as in the case of industrial poisons (mercury, carbon monoxide, lead), powerful modern medicines (cortisone, sulfonamides), and specific vitamin deficiencies. (Wernicke's encephalopathy, pellagra). Similarly, the curandero has no knowledge of the tie-in of the toxemias of pregnancy with mental retardation nor can he cope with head injuries brought about by trauma.

A second grouping contains those serious disorders such as

schizophrenia and the manic-depressive psychoses which, while classed as functional disorders, are nevertheless probably more likely to be caused or complicated by a basic biochemical or physiological lesion. This grouping is comprised of a number of disorders of as yet undetermined etiology. For the most severe of these disorders, dementia praecox, the curandero is no better or worse than his modern counterpart. He has no specific treatment for this, although it seems likely that the subculture's more supportive and tolerant attitude, coupled with its lack of emphasis on achievement orientation, makes it likely that such cases might not deteriorate as badly as in the urban United States. Similarly, the social disability syndromes grafted onto underlying severe psychiatric disorders are less likely to be induced by the kind of treatment given by the curandero and carried through by the patients' families.

However, for acute psychotic disorders of mood and thought (depression and schizophrenia) the curandero is less well equipped than the contemporary psychiatrist. He does not have available the powerful tranquilizing or antidepressant drugs that have proven so effective in the management and treatment of the severe disorders. Here too, as in the case of the first group of disorders, scientific developments in psychiatry that have occurred simultaneously, but independently of the growth and development of the dynamic psychotherapies clearly differentiate the folk from the modern treatment.

For the less severe psychoses, such as the mild paranoid reactions and the ambulatory schizophrenic reactions, there is good reason to suggest that the curandero's approach is more effective or as effective for his patients as the psychotherapist's is for his. Most important is that the patient feel comfortable and reassured by a healer who does not intrude on his psychological space, i.e., is not too seductive and threatening.

For the obsessive compulsive neuroses and psychopathic disorders that are notoriously resistant to psychotherapy, the curandero brings no special strengths or skills. He does not have a better way to influence the abreaction of emotion in the obsessional nor to introduce into the psychopath an ability to tolerate frustration and an inclination to act in a way respectful of society. For the obsessional with the severe superego restraints, he cannot relax the superego pressure. Similarly, for the conscienceless psychopath, he cannot induce a sense of guilt.

Finally, there are the less severe or neurotic disorders, which are related to interpersonal social and cultural stress interacting with personality patterns and conflicts. It is in relationship to this last category that both curanderismo and dynamic psychotherapy must be considered. The relative merits of curanderismo and dynamic psychotherapy in the treatment of neurotic disorders vary with the type and severity of the disorder. These differences are illustrated in a consideration of the treatment of the depressive disorders, on the one hand, and of the milder characterological or existential disorders of alienated modern man, on the other. The curandero's approach would appear to be better suited for the depressed patient providing as it does reassurance, support, and the promise of help. Most crucial, the patient can hope for improvement by virtue of the faith he sets in the curandero. In contrast to this, the dynamic psychotherapeutic treatment of depressive disorders tends often to have serious consequences for the patient. The detailed inquiry into emotionally charged areas of the patient's life and the attempt to assist the patient in gaining insight may intensify guilt and anxiety and make the already guilt-ridden patient more depressed. Assigning responsibility to the patient who already feels excessively responsible, even for things he hasn't done, may make him feel even worse.

Autonomy, initiative, and independence are of value in the urban setting where the isolated individual must rely less upon traditional patterns and beliefs and more upon himself. Dynamic psychotherapy, which strives for such goals, may not be useful for very troubled people since it encourages patients to give up traditional beliefs and "ur-defenses," which few people can do without. In addition, many patients have guilt and anxiety about freeing themselves from primary family ties and relationships and are made more anxious by dynamic psychotherapy.

However, in the treatment of patients who are functioning adequately and in whom the goal of treatment is permanent and lasting personality change, dynamic psychotherapy is eminently more suitable than curanderismo. Once a patient is functioning, he needs less of the support and reassurance of the therapist and can be confronted with ways in which he is doing things and what must be changed for his relationships to improve. Thus, once security is obtained, the patient can begin his search for greater personal freedom. The encouragement of independent behavior, however, is anxiety-provoking, since the individual must take responsibility for his behavior and must be willing to act in a nonhabitual way, which provokes anxiety and requires faith and courage. The therapist's task is to provide sufficient motivation through his persuasiveness so that the patient will attempt to try the new. The establishment of an intense dependency relationship and the manipulation of this dependency to encourage the patient to change—by giving up accustomed ways of doing things—is the key feature of dynamic psychotherapy.

In addition to subscribing to a markedly different theoretical and empirical approach from that of Anglo psychiatrists, the curandero follows a number of other patterns, which are perhaps significant in helping to perpetuate reliance on his methods even when more modern methods are available. The curandero, unlike the Anglo psychiatrist, treats the patient in the presence of his family, never in an impersonal clinic or hospital situation. The curandero, unlike the psychiatrist, also permits the head of the family—usually the father—to decide whether and when treatment should be initiated, and permits the family to participate to an active extent in the course of treatment, which usually takes place before the altar in the curandero's home. The Mexican-American group do not put as much stress on privacy and individual responsibility as do the Anglos, and thus have great difficulty in accepting hospitalization and the prohibitions on hospital visiting.

Furthermore, the curandero recognizes and treats folk illnesses such as *susto, ojo,* and *embrujada,* while physicians, who do not believe in such illnesses, cannot reinforce the Mexicans' beliefs nor provide them with necessary support. Curanderos are also more sensitive to and capable of handling the social crises associated with folk illnesses, as well as the particular anxieties associated with certain kinds of illnesses which have much meaning for the Mexicans.

Often the anxiety associated with the meaning of illness is an important determinant of whether an individual seeks treatment and what kind of treatment he seeks. This problem is clearly seen in the case of tuberculosis, which can make Anglo patients very anxious even when they are not symptomatically ill. The Mexican does not become anxious because he does not know very much about this illness, particularly if he is symptom free or has only minimal symptoms. (Foster, 1951) He is not as likely to seek help for a symptomatic tuberculosis as he is, for example, for a severe case of indigestion which frightens him. The physician who cannot recognize the cultural and symbolic sources of anxiety among Mexican-American patients cannot provide them with the necessary anxiety reducing measures.

Physicians are inclined to prescribe specific treatments for specific ailments, or nothing when there are no adequate treatment measures, as in the case of a viral influenza. By contrast, the curandero pays much attention to the patient's emotional state and will often provide elaborate treatment for medically minor problems that have much anxiety associated with them. By taking the patient's problems seriously and not readily dispensing reassurance, the curandero instills much confidence in his patients. American doctors, in contrast, traditionally reassure by minimizing the seriousness of the patient's problem. Furthermore, while the medically trained individual will attribute his successes to the medicines he uses, the curandero will maximize his personal significance in treatment.

Patients accustomed to such treatment are often disappointed by physicians who minimize their own participation in the treatment process and who treat them in line with a scientific, universalistic, technologcal orientation where objectivity and impersonality are the preferred approaches.

The curandero is never in doubt as to the diagnosis or treatment and does not undermine confidence in himself among nontechnically oriented patients by ordering laboratory tests and X-rays. He turns to meaningful sources of strength such as the saints and God.

The aspects of medical procedure that arouse confidence are clearly conditioned by culturally meaningful symbols. Even when taking the initial history, the curandero conveys the impression that he already knows the answer and wants only further clarification.

When curanderos prophesy and predict the future, patients with doubts and anxieties are often comforted. In contrast to these predictions, the wait-and-see attitude of many physicians is often inadequate to meet the needs of the Mexican patient. The curandero's inclination to dramatize his predictions also helps in allaying anxiety. Coming from a society which emphasizes interpersonal relations, the Mexican-American does not value a doctor's ability because of the doctor's apparent material success or technological competence, but is more concerned with the way in which he and his family are treated. This concern often gives the curandero more influence than the medical school graduate. The curandero's association with religious beliefs and practices adds further to his appeal.

In that curanderismo occurs within the context of other social relationships and not in a separated and highly specialized form of relationship ordered by universalistic, rational, and scientific criteria, it meets certain needs of the Mexican patient which modern Western medicine, with its notions of privacy, cannot.

Epilogue

WORK IN ETHNOPSYCHIATRY has only just begun. The studies in *Magic, Faith, and Healing* (ed. by Ari Kiev, 1964) led to the recognition of prescientific psychiatries and the relationship of these to each other and to contemporary psychotherapy. In this book we have gone further in more explicitly examining the tie-in of cultural factors with both illness and treatment procedures. Most important, we have obtained a firmer notion of the therapeutic significance of culture-specific factors.

More remains to be done both with regard to the systematic gathering of data and the setting of testable hypotheses within the framework of existing theories. More descriptive information is needed from various groups. It would be of interest to know the distribution of treatment techniques and the relationship of this distribution to the distribution of various disorders in various cultural groups throughout the world. Such epidemiological analyses, however, will not be forthcoming until better epidemiological techniques are devised. Long-term follow-up studies of cases treated by various techniques are also needed, although it is doubtful that they can be done until better means for measuring the effects of contemporary treatments are devised. Thus, many of the questions and challenges that may be posed to the primitive treatments depend upon the development of methods useful for examining these questions.

Even though definitive studies of the efficacy and relative merits of different forms of treatment cannot yet be done, there is much to argue for further such descriptive, analytic studies as the present one. The most important reason for additional study is to increase our understanding of the various ways in which help can be rendered to persons suffering from mental illness. There is a tendency for culture to be constrictive and encouraging of the repetitive use of certain patterns and practices, oftentimes to the exclusion of those which formerly were useful.

Curanderismo has implications for the larger question of social change and mental illness. Curanderismo, like other forms of folk treatment, appears to be one factor accounting for the low incidence of psychiatric disorders in societies undergoing considerable social change, where rates would be expected to be higher. Individuals moving into urban areas bereft of their tribal ties lose not only their sense of identity and their bearings but also traditional ritualistic means of anxiety reduction, with the result that in many urban areas one finds increased mental illness as well as increased crime, alcoholism, delinquency, and other forms of social breakdown.

The resurgence or continued use of folk practices in various parts of the developing world of Asia, Africa and South America may account for some reduction in the rates of psychiatric disorder encountered in these societies. Indeed many disturbed people may be able to make a marginal out-of-hospital adjustment by total involvement in sects or in various kinds of movements.

The significance of cultural factors is further highlighted by perpetuation of folkways in the face of rapid social change. Although the curandero must now seek regular employment, he continues to be preferred over modern experts as a source of psychological help for many Mexican-Americans. Cultural factors thus play an important role in the acceptance or rejection of Western ideas and practices and must be thoroughly considered if problems are to be avoided when introducing Western concepts of hygiene, disease prevention, and treatment to less developed areas or "less fortunate" subcultures. Often, what has been thought to be of "scientific" value has in the end proven to be of cultural origin only.

A close look at curanderismo reveals the presence of many elements ordinarily found in contemporary psychotherapy, elements which are beneficial in resolving the manifest conflicts of individuals and in providing corrective emotional experiences. The curanderismo complex also acts in a preventive way, as regards both the minor and the major psychiatric disorders. It provides a number of things that enable individuals to resolve tensions and thereby to prevent development of disorders. It provides those with disorders such as chronic schizophrenia a kind of social support that enables them to continue to function in a supportive atmosphere. Thus it serves prophylactic purposes. When these practices are no longer available, individuals who previously were able to cope are no longer able. Curanderismo is also important not only as a form of prevention which contributes to lower incidence, but as a form of treatment agency whose presence leads to a reduced flow of people going to hospitals.

Bibliography

Ackerknecht, Erwin H., "Primitive Medicine's Social Function," Paul Rivers (ed.), *Miscellania,* Mexico, 1958.

Barrett, Donald N. & Julian Samora, "The Movement of Spanish Youth From Rural to Urban Settings." Paper presented at the National Conference on Problems of Rural Youth in a Changing Environment, September, 1963, Washington, D.C.

Beltran, Gonzalo Aguirre, *Medicina Y Magia,* Instituto Nacional Indigenista, Mexico City, 1963.

Benedict, Ruth, "Anthropology and the Abnormal," Journal of Genetic Psychology, 10:59–82, 1934.

Bleuler, E. P., *Dementia Praecox or the Group of Schizophrenias,* trans by J. Zinkin, International Universities Press, New York, 1950.

Bourke, John H., Popular "Medicine Customs and Superstitions of the Rio Grande," Journal of American Folklore, 7 :119–146, 1894.

Boyer, L. Bryce, "Folk Psychiatry of the Apaches of the Mescalero Indian Reservation," *Magic, Faith, and Healing,* Ari Kiev (ed.), The Free Press, New York, 1964.

Boyer, R. M., (1962) "Social Structure and Socialization Among the Apache of the Mescalero Indian Reservation." Unpublished Ph.D. dissertation, University of California.

Burma, John H., (1954) *Spanish Speaking Groups in the United States,* Duke University Press, Durham.

Carothers, J. C., (1953) *The African Mind in Health and Disease,* World Health Organization, Monograph series, No. 17, Geneva, 1953.

Castiglioni, Arturo, (1958) *A History of Medicine,* trans from the Italian and edited by E. B. Krumbhaar, 2nd ed., rev., Knopf, New York.

Caudill, William, (1949) "Psychological Characteristics of Acculturated Wisconsin Ojibwa Children," *American Anthropologist,* 51 : 409–27.

Clark, Margaret, *Health in the Mexican-American Community, A Community Study,* University of California Press, Berkeley, California, 1959.

Cline, Howard, (1963) *Mexico : Revolution to Evolution, 1940–60,* Oxford University Press, New York.

Curtin, L. S. M., (1947) *Healing Herbs of the Upper Rio Grande,* Laboratory of Anthropology, Santa Fe.

Devereux, George, (1951) *Reality and Dream, Psychotherapy of a Plains Indian,* International University Press, New York.

——— (1956) "Normal and Abnormal : The Key Problems of Psychiatric Anthropolgy," J. B. Casagande and T. Gladwin (eds.), *Some Uses of Anthropology : Theoretical and Applied,* Anthropological Society of Washington, Washington, D.C.

——— (1958) "Cultural Thought Models in Primitive and Modern Psychiatric Theories," *Psychiatry,* 21 :359–74.

——— (1961) *Mohave Ethnopsychiatry and Suicide : The Psychiatric Knowledge and the Psychic Disturbances of an Indian*

Tribe, Bureau of American Ethnology Bulletin No. 175, The Smithsonian Institution, Washington, D.C.

Diaz-Guerrero, Rogelio, (1955) "Neurosis and the Mexican Family Structure," *American Journal of Psychiatry,* 112 :411–17.

Edmondson, Munro S., (1957) *A Triangulation on the Culture of Mexico,* American Research Institution, Tulane University, 205–40, New Orleans.

Erasmus, Charles John, (1952) "Changing Folk Beliefs and the Relativity of Empirical Knowledge," *Southwestern Journal of Anthropology,* 8 :411–28.

Erikson, E. H., (1950) *Childhood and Society,* W. W. Norton & Company, New York.

——— (1958) *Young Man Luther,* W. W. Norton & Company, New York.

Evans-Pritchard, E., (1937) *Witchcraft, Oracles and Magic Among Azande,* Oxford University Press, London.

Farris, Buford E. & Wm. M. Hale, (1963) "Mexican-American Conflict Gangs," Research and Educational Reports No. 1, Wesley Community Centers, San Antonio, Texas.

Fenichel, Otto, (1945) *The Psychoanalytic Theory of Neurosis,* W. W. Norton & Co., New York.

——— (1955) "Brief Psychotherapy," Collected Papers, 2nd series, Routledge and Kegan Paul, Ltd., London, 243–59.

Fish, F. J., (1962) *Schizophrenia,* Williams and Wilkins, Baltimore.

Fisher, C., (1953) "Studies on the Nature of Suggestions : Part I of Experimental Induction of Dreams by Direct Suggestion," *Journal of the American Psychoanalytic Association,* 1 :222–55.

Foster, George (ed.), (1951) "A Cross-Culture Anthropological Analysis of a Technical Aid Program," The Smithsonian Institution, Washington, D.C.

——— (1953) "Cofradia & Compadrazgo in Spain and Spanish America," *Southwestern Journal of Anthropology,* 9 :1–28.

Fox, Robin, (1964) "Witchcraft and Clanship in Cochiti Therapy," *Magic, Faith, And Healing,* in Ari Kiev (ed.), The Free Press, New York.

Frank, Jerome D., (1961) *Persuasion and Healing,* Johns Hopkins Press, Baltimore.

Freud, Sigmund, (1959) "On Psychotherapy," *Collected Papers,* Basic Books, New York, 1 :249–63.

Gillin, John, (1948) "Magical Fright," *Psychiatry,* 2 :387–400.

———— (1955) "Ethos Components in Modern Latin American Culture," *American Anthropologist,* 47 :489–501.

———— (1957) "Cross-Cultural Aspects of Socio-Cultural Therapy," *Progress in Psychotherapy,* 2 :224–30.

Greenson, Ralph R., (1959) "The Classic Psychoanalytic Approach," *American Handbook of Psychiatry,* Silvano Arieti (ed.), Basic Books, New York, 2 :1399–1416.

Hallowell, A. I., (1934) "Culture and Mental Disorder," *Journal of Abnormal and Social Psychology,* 29 :1–9.

———— (1936) "Psychic Stresses and Culture Patterns," *American Journal of Psychiatry,* 92 :1291–1310.

———— (1938) "Fear and Anxiety as Cultural and Individual Variables in a Primitive Society," *Journal of Social Psychology,* 9 :24–27.

Hawley, Florence & Donovan Senter, (1946) "Group-Designed Behavior Patterns in Two Acculturating Groups," *Southwestern Journal of Anthropology,* 2 :133–51.

Holland, William R. & Roland G. Tharp (1964) "Highland Maya Psychotherapy," *American Anthropologist,* 66 :41–52.

Hudson, William M. (ed.), (1951) *The Healer of Los Olmos and Other Mexican Lore,* Texas Folklore Society Publication 24, Southern Methodist University Press, Dallas.

Hurt, Wesley R., Jr., (1940) "Witchcraft in New Mexico," *El Palacio,* 47 :73–96.

Iturriaga, Jose E., (1951) *La Estructura Social y Cultural de Mexico,* Mexico City : Fondo de Cultura Economica. Cited in John P. Gillin, "Some Signposts for Policy," *Social Change in Latin America Today,* Vintage, New York (1960), 14–62.

Jaspers, Karl, (1964) *General Psychopathology,* University of Chicago Press, Chicago.

Jones, Ernest, (1923) "The God Complex," in *Essays in Applied Psychoanalysis*, International Psychoanalytic Press, London.

Kardiner, Abram, Ralph D. Linton, Cora DuBois, & J. West, (1945) *The Psychological Frontiers of Society*, Columbia University Press, New York.

Kibbe, Pauline R., (1946) *Latin Americans in Texas*, University of New Mexico Press, p 302, Santa Fe.

Kiev, Ari, (1961) "Primitive Therapy : A Cross-Cultural Study of the Relationship Between Child Training and Therapeutic Practices Related to Illness," Muensterberger, W. & Sidney Axelrod (eds.), *Psychoanalytic Study of Society I*, International Universities Press, New York, 185–217.

—— (1963) "Community Psychiatry : Observations of Recent English Developments," *Comprehensive Psychiatry*, 4 :291–97.

—— (1963) "Some Background Factors in Recent English Psychiatric Progress"; American Journal of Psychiatry, 119 :851–56.

—— (1964) "Psychiatric Nosology : American and British Trends," *Canadian Psychiatric Association Journal*, 9 :114–19.

—— (1964) "Impressions of English Psychiatric Training With Special Reference to Postgraduate Training," *Comprehensive Psychiatry*, 5 :67–73.

—— (ed.), (1964) *Magic, Faith, and Healing: Studies in Primitive Psychiatry Today*, The Free Press, New York.

Klapp, Orrin E., (1964) "Mexican Social Types," *American Journal of Sociology*, 69 :404–14.

Kubie, Lawrence Schlesinger, *Practical and Theoretical Aspects of Psychoanalysis*, International Universities Press, 1950, New York.

LaBarre, Weston, (1947) "Primitive Psychotherapy in Native American Cultures : Peyotism and Confession," *Journal of Abnormal and Social Psychology*, 42 :294–309.

Landes, Ruth, (1938) "The Abnormal Among the Ojibwa Indians," *Journal of Abnormal and Social Psychology*, 33 :14–33.

Lewis, Oscar, (1963) *Life in a Mexican Village: Tepoztlan Restudied*, University of Illinois Press, Urbana, 512.

Loeb, E., (1929) "Shaman and Seer," *American Anthropologist*, 31.

Loomis, Charles, & Leonard Olen, (1941) *Culture of a Contemporary Rural Community, El Cerrito, New Mexico,* Bureau of Agricultural Economics, U.S.D.A. Rural Life Studies No. 1, Washington.

Madsen, William, (1964a.) "The Alcoholic Agringado." Unpublished paper. *American Anthropolist,* 66 : 355–61.

———— (1955) "Hot and Cold in the Universe of San Francisco Tecospa Valley of Mexico," *Journal of American Folklore,* 68 : 123–29.

———— (1957) *Christo-Paganism,* Middle American Research Institute, Tulane University, 19 : 105–80, New Orleans.

———— (1961) "Society and Health in the Lower Rio Grande Valley : A Guide for Medical and Welfare Workers Among the Mexican-American," The Hogg Foundation for Mental Health, Austin, Texas, 1961.

———— (1964) "Value Conflicts and Folk Psychotherapy in South Texas," in *Magic, Faith, and Healing,* Ari Kiev (ed.), The Free Press, New York, 420–40.

Malinowski, Bronislaw, (1948) *Magic, Science, and Religion, and Other Essays,* The Free Press, New York.

Mannheim, Karl, (1936) *Ideology and Utopia,* Harvest Books, New York.

Mead, Margaret (ed.), (1953) *Cultural Patterns and Technical Change,* UNESCO, Paris.

Menninger, Karl, (1963) *The Vital Balance,* Viking Press, New York.

Meyer, A., (1951) *The Collected Papers of Adolf Meyer, Vol. II Psychiatry,* John Hopkins Press, Baltimore.

Opler, M. K., (1956) *Culture, Psychiatry, and Human Values,* Charles C. Thomas, Springfield.

Parsons, Elsie Clews, (1927) "Witchcraft Among the Pueblos : Indian or Spanish?", *Man.* London, 27 : 106–29.

Parsons, Talcott, (1951) "Illness and the Role of the Physician," *American Journal Orthopsychiatry,* 21 : 452–60.

———— (1951) "Social Structure and Dynamic Process : The Case of Modern Medical Practice in the Social System," The Free Press, New York.

Paul, Benjamin D., (1958) "The Role of Beliefs and Customs in Sanitation Programs," *American Journal of Public Health,* 48 : 1502–1506.

Paz, Octavio, (1961) *The Labyrinth of Solitude,* Grove Press, New York.

Prescott, William Hickling, (1936) *History of the Conquest of Mexico, and of the Conquest of Peru,* The Modern Library, New York.

Prince, Raymond, (1964) "Indigenous Yoruba Psychiatry," in *Magic, Faith, and Healing,* Ari Kiev (ed.), The Free Press, New York, 84–118.

Radcliffe-Brown, A. R., (1952) *Structure and Function in Primitive Society,* The Free Press, New York.

Ramirez, Santiago & Ramon Parres, (1957) "Some Dynamic Patterns in the Organization of the Mexican Family," *International Journal of Social Psychiatry,* 3 :18–21.

Ramos, Samuel, (1962) *Profile of Man and Culture in Mexico,* University of Texas Press, Austin, Texas.

Rogers, Carl, (1942) *Counseling and Psychotherapy,* Houghton Mifflin, Boston.

Romano, Octavio Ignacio, (1960) "Donship in a Mexican-American Community in Texas," *American Anthropologist,* 62 :966–77.

Rubel, Arthur J., (1960) "Concepts of Disease in Mexican-American Community in Texas," *American Anthropologist,* 62 :795–814.

Sahagun, Bernardino, (1946) *Historia General de las Coas de Nueva Espana Editorial Nueva Espana S.A.,* Mexico 1 :472–77. Cited in Laurette Sejourne, *Burning Water, Thought and Religion in Ancient Mexico,* The Vanguard Press, New York, 1956.

Sanseigne, Alain & Max Desrosiers, (1961) "The Evaluation for Psychopharmaceuticals in an Underdeveloped Country," in N.S. Kline (ed.) *Psychiatry in the Underdeveloped Countries,* American Psychiatric Association, Washington, D.C., 52–58.

Saunders, Lyle, (1954) *Cultural Difference and Medical Care : The*

Case for the Spanish Speaking People of the Southwest, Russell Sage Foundation, New York.

Schulman, Sam & Anne M. Smith, (1962) "Health and Disease in Northern New Mexico : A Research Report." Unpublished typescript, University of Colorado, Boulder.

Senter, Donovan, (1945) "Acculturation Among New Mexican Villagers in Comparison to Adjustment Patterns of Other Spanish-Speaking Americans," *Rural Sociology,* 1 : 32–47.

——— (1947) "Witches and Psychiatrists," *Psychiatry,* 10 : 49–56.

Sereno, Renzo, (1948) "Obeah; Magic and Social Structure in the Lesser Antilles," *Psychiatry,* 2 : 15–31.

Simmons, Leo & H. G. Wolff, (1954) *Social Science in Medicine,* Russell Sage Foundation, New York.

Simmons, Ozzie G., (1961) "The Mutual Images and Expectations of Anglo-Americans and Mexican-Americans," *Daedalus,* 286–99. Spring, 1961.

Smithers, W. D., (1963) "Nature's Pharmacy and the Curanderos," *Sul Ross State College Bulletin,* 41 No. 3, West Texas Historical and Scientific Society, Alpine, Texas.

Tawney, Richard Henry, (1926) *Religion and the Rise of Capitalism,* Harcourt, Brace and World, New York.

Tuck, Ruth, (1946) *Not With the Fist,* Harcourt, Brace and World, New York.

Van der Eerden, Sister M. Lucia, S.C.M.M., (1948) *Maternity Care in a Spanish-American Community of New Mexico,* Catholic University of America Press, Washington, D.C.

Whiting, J. W. M. & Irvin L. Child, (1953) *Child Training and Personality : A Cross-Cultural Study,* Yale University Press, New Haven.

Yap, P. M., (1951) "Mental Diseases Peculiar to Certain Cultures : A Survey of Comparative Psychiatry," *Journal of Mental Science,* 97 : 313–27.

Zilboorg, Gregory and George Henry, (1941) *A History of Medical Psychology,* W. W. Norton & Company, New York.

Index